Bobby Flay's

Bold American Food

Bobby Flay's

WARNER BOOKS

A Time Warner Company

Bold American Food

Food

More than **200** Revolutionary Recipes

By Bobby Flay with Joan Schwartz

Photographs by Tom Eckerle   +   Design by Stark Design

Dedicated to

My mother, Dorothy Flay,
who is always cheering for her son

My father, Bill Flay,
who taught me to do the right thing in business and in life

My grandmother, Mary Flay

And in memory of my grandfather, Willie Flay,
the man I take after

Grateful acknowledgment is made for permission to use the following recipes, which are reprinted, adapted, or derived from the sources below.

Chipotle Brioche, Stephan Pyles, author, *The New Texas Cuisine*
Black Rice, Kevin Rathbun
Southwestern Ceviche, Jonathan Waxman
Chocolate Polenta Soufflé Cake, Amir Ilan
Apricot Serrano Chile Sauce, Katy Sparks
Mesa Grill Dinner Rolls, Wayne Brachman

Grateful acknowledgment to Izabel Lam International, Swid-Powell, and Zona for their kind assistance.

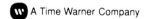 A Time Warner Company

Printed in Japan
First Printing: May 1994
10 9 8 7 6 5 4 3 2
Library of Congress Cataloging–in–Publication Data
Flay, Bobby.
Bobby Flay's Bold American food: more than 200 revolutionary
recipes / Bobby Flay, with Joan Schwartz.
p. cm.
Includes index.
ISBN 0-446-51724-0
1. Cookery, American–Southwestern style. I. Schwartz, Joan
1938– . II. Title.
TX715.2.S69F57 1994   93-6342
641.5979—dc20   CIP

Many people have been important to me and to this book...

First, my thanks and love to Debra Ponzek.

Thanks to my partners at Mesa Grill, Jerry Kretchmer, Jeff Bliss, and Laurence Kretchmer, for opening the restaurant that I always dreamed of and for making it so wholeheartedly a team effort; to Lynn Loflin and Rich Kresberg, owners of Miracle Grill, who gave my career a great start; and to Paul Del Favero and Gail Arnold, who grew up with me in the business.

Thanks to the people I count on every day, who shared in this book: Fran Bernfeld, who has worked with me since the first day at Miracle Grill, and consistently keeps the customers happy; my sous-chefs—Katy Sparks, another Mesa pioneer, who keeps everything running even when I am not there; Jan Sendel, whose ambition and focus inspire the kitchen; and Larry Manheim, whose great palate I relied on; Wayne Brachman, pastry chef, who helped with bread and dessert recipes; Patricia Yeo, my sous-chef for three years, who helped me to form this cuisine; Debby Goldman, my first "good customer"; and Jerry and Janet Silverstein, for all their support and encouragement.

I will always be grateful to Joe Allen, New York restaurateur, who started it all by giving me my first job and sending me to school, where I discovered a new world.

Thanks to Jonathan Waxman, the first person to show me what good food was, and to Larry Forgione, who has been there to help and advise; to Stephan Pyles, Robert Del Grande, Dean Fearing, and Kevin Rathbun, the true innovators in this cuisine—I am happy to follow their lead.

Thanks to Jack McDavid, who taught me the importance of freshness and quality, and to Ed Brown, my seafood guide. Whenever I have a food question, they have the answer.

I am grateful to Gael Greene, Florence Fabricant, Jane Freiman, and Bryan Miller, the New York food press, for understanding my food and for consistently supporting it, and to Arlene Feltman Sailhac, who invited me to teach at De Gustibus at Macy's and gave me valuable exposure.

I'm grateful to my friends in Texas who brought me to the source: Ed and Susan Auler, of Fall Creek Vineyard; Ann Clark, writer and teacher; Paula Lambert, of The Mozzarella Company in Dallas; and Karen MacNeil, who introduced me to the people and the ideas.

My gratitude to Liv Blumer, full-time editor and part-time recipe tester, who first saw the possibility of this book, and to Harvey-Jane Kowal, for combining editing skill with good humor; to Jane Dystel, super-agent, whose energy, talent, and imagination carried me over many hurdles; to Tom Eckerle and Ceci Gallini, who made the pages look delicious; to Adriane Stark, for her clear and imaginative design; to Bernadette Cura, for her valuable assistance throughout the photo shoots; and to Joan Schwartz, without whom there wouldn't be a book, for sure.

Finally, thanks to Patrick O'Brien, my best friend, who has always had confidence in my visions.

acknowledgments

table of contents

growing up rebellious and hell-raising in New York City wasn't exactly the right training for a chef who would one day celebrate the food of the American Southwest. Or was it? Sometimes I think my younger days have had a direct influence on the way I cook. My food is straightforward, but impulsive and almost always explosive—pretty much like my old street gang. As a kid, I broke the rules and took a lot of chances, but I always seemed to know where I was going. At some point, and I'm not really sure how, I changed direction. I stopped making trouble and began concentrating on my life. I managed to turn fearless negative energy into fearless positive energy.

What was my path from troublemaker to chef? I sort of fell into cooking at the age of seventeen, when my father got me a job at Joe Allen's Restaurant in New York City's theater district. At first, it was just a job that he demanded I take, a last chance for a decent life. School wasn't my first love and probably not my second, either, so he made it clear that I had to work. But I didn't take to regimentation very well. I remember the days when my father would be waiting in front of the restaurant when I was an hour or so late for work. Just thinking about it still sends chills down my spine.

But after a while, when I realized that I enjoyed what I was doing, I went full speed into my new occupation and astonished everyone. I began to dream of a serious restaurant career, and Joe Allen was generous enough to pay my tuition to the French Culinary Institute. It was exciting to be in the school's first class, although there were many other moments when the wise guy whispered in my ear, "Oh, no, not back to school. Forget it!"

But this school was different from any I had been to before—it held my interest. When I graduated from FCI in 1984 at the age of twenty, I became the first chef of a neighborhood restaurant called Brighton Grill. That job was a whirlwind experience, both good and bad. It was good because it gave me a chance to be creative and to learn how to relate to other creative people, bad because I felt young, inexperienced, and insecure. While my heart was in it 110 percent, I must admit I was in a little over my head.

My next job was the turning point in my cooking career. Jonathan Waxman had recently arrived from Los Angeles and had opened Jams, the hottest restaurant in New York, followed by Bud's, probably the second hottest. One night I was at a cocktail party at the FCI, and I met Gail Arnold, the chef at Bud's and a great friend to this day. Five minutes into our conversation, Gail offered me a job as a line cook, and I accepted. At Bud's I got the chance to work with incredible cooks, most of whom have gone on to open their own restaurants. They used ingredients that were on the cutting edge and were the freshest and best that money could buy. They introduced me to blue corn tortillas, poblano peppers, ancho chiles, mangoes, papayas, black beans, tomatillos, and cilantro. They showed me that there could be real excitement and pride in American food.

From Bud's, I went to Hulot's, a neighborhood French bistro that Jonathan Waxman opened. There I got to know Stephanie Lyness and Paul Del Favero, the chef and sous-chef, respectively. Stephanie ran the kitchen magnificently, and I have yet to meet anyone who cooks with more passion than Paul. It was Paul who helped me hone my basic French culinary skills. We still try to cook together either socially or professionally as much as we can.

After a couple of career "experiments," eventually I was hired as the chef of a new Southwestern restaurant called Miracle Grill. The owners, Rich Kresberg and Lynn Loflin, went along with even my wildest suggestions. It took a few months for the restaurant to get off the ground, but when it took off, it flew.

More and more, I began to think about the direction this cuisine could take, and the wide acceptance it was bound to have. Ever since my days at Joe Allen's, I had been imagining the perfect restaurant, a soaring space on a lively street. It would incorporate all I had learned about food and all I was inventing. It would have an exciting all-American wine list. I got the break when Jerry Kretchmer, who also owns Gotham Bar and Grill and One Fifth Avenue, asked me to be his partner in a restaurant venture.

Mesa Grill, which we opened in January 1991, is the restaurant I dreamed about back in my days at Joe Allen's and Miracle Grill. It's an expression of my attitude toward food and life. I call it "serious fun." Behind the exciting, playful food, there is a strong vision of American cuisine.

Bold and *sizzling* are the two words that best describe the food I cook. Bold ingredients like fresh and dried chile peppers; garlic that is sautéed, roasted, or toasted; tart tomatillos, cranberries, and limes are all used for accent, not injury. (Spicy, to me, means flavorful and well balanced; it doesn't mean burn-your-mouth-out.) Full-flavored herbaceous sauces, made from fresh cilantro, basil, sage, or oregano extend the range.

Sizzling is not only the sound of a basil and roasted jalapeño vinaigrette hitting a hot-off-the-grill black sea bass or salmon steak, it stands for the distinctive colors and textures that are so much a part of my food. In each dish, I like to use three or four sizzling flavors, colors, and textures, any of which can stand alone, but which are sensational when combined. A perfect example is grilled tuna atop a crisp flour tortilla, served with glistening black bean–mango salsa and an electric-green avocado vinaigrette.

The great thing about cooking this way is that when you put something into a dish, you still recognize it at the end. Each ingredient comes through clearly. The elements don't melt together; they all bounce off each other, and you get a lot of flavors and textures, singing up the scale and down.

If you have been to Mesa Grill, you will recognize the recipes that follow, all of which have been on the menu at one time or another. I've picked my favorites and have reworked them to make sense in your kitchen. You can buy the major ingredients in supermarkets, and the Southwestern specialties, like fresh chiles and tortillas, in Hispanic markets and by mail (page 205). Many Southwestern foods are becoming mainstream, and you may be surprised at their availability in your neighborhood. Making Southwestern food accessible is the real point of this book, and I believe I have done that.

Fresh salsas and relishes, salads, seasonal vegetables, and grilled and roasted fish, poultry, and meat make this a light cuisine. But there are exceptions, there's no getting around it. Some of my gratins and desserts require heavy cream. Nothing else will work. As long as you don't do three of those recipes at the same time, you'll be fine. A small portion of your dinner will contain more fat than the other parts. Just be aware of that.

Although my recipes are precise, this isn't a rule book—at some point, your own spontaneity will kick in, and you'll cook the food your way, to suit your taste. Just remember to use the boldest ingredients you can find, make your food sizzle, and enjoy it all.

Bobby Flay, *New York City*

ingredients +

techniques +

equipment

1

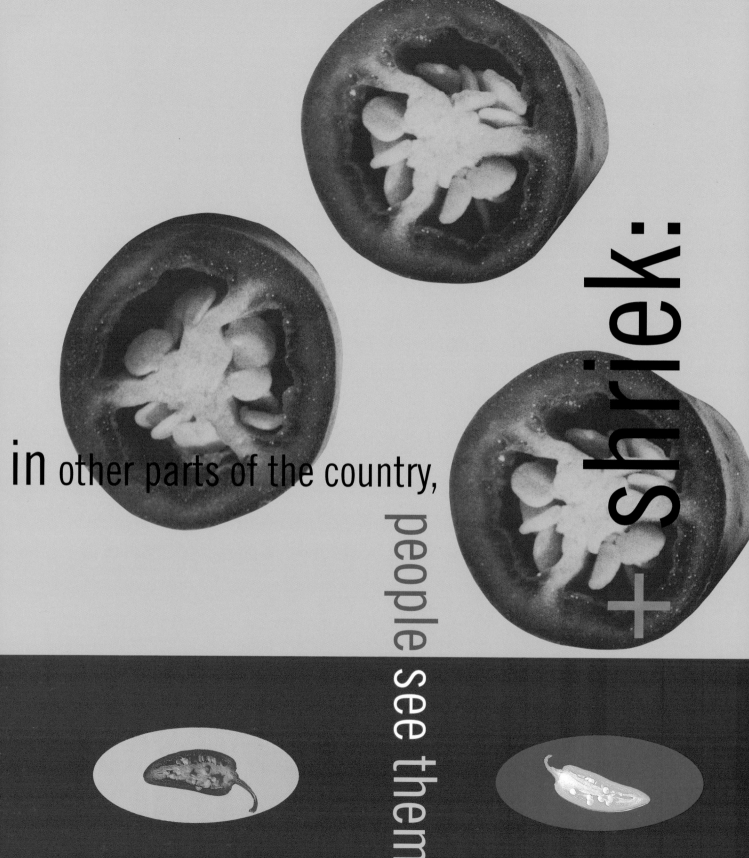

in other parts of the country,

people see them

+ shriek:

My God,

what

am I
going to do with

these

In Southwestern kitchens, cooks are doing what comes naturally: smoking, roasting, and grilling the foods they have grown up with. Ingredients that seem exotic to many of us are commonplace in Texas, New Mexico, and Arizona. And they are, after all, pretty simple—what could be simpler than chile peppers? But in other parts of the country, people see them and wonder, "My God, what am I going to do with these? Do I chop them? Do I roast them? How many do I use?"

Southwestern Americans are surrounded by great foods. On my last visit to Texas for the annual Texas Hill Country Food and Wine Festival, a local chef asked me, "What kind of food do you cook in New York?" When I told him "Southwestern," it blew his mind! To him, Southwestern food is anything anybody happens to cook in the Southwest; it is not a cuisine.

To me, though, it is a cuisine. I began cooking this food because I really liked the ingredients—the fresh green flavors of chiles, along with their sometimes subtle and sometimes stunning heat; the sweetness and aromas of ripe fruits and vegetables; and the pungency of fresh herbs. All the dishes I created grew out of the Southwestern ingredients listed below. Since I first started cooking with them, my repertoire has evolved. Some ingredients have become more important and others have been discarded. These are foods that work perfectly together, and they are truly American foods.

Ingredients

ingredients, techniques & equipment

CHILES

Chiles seem to frighten otherwise brave people, who handle them hesitantly and worry that they'll be too hot. There is an easy, one-word answer to that problem: balance. If you have given a dish too much heat, you can easily add a touch of maple syrup or honey or a chunk of sweet fruit like mango or papaya to soften or balance it. They will bring harmony and complexity to the finished dish.

I walk around my restaurant kitchen tasting the sauces and salsas that my staff puts together, and I say, "This is too spicy; balance it with mango," or "This isn't spicy enough; add some chipotles to fire it up." You can always create a balance. It's no more difficult than finishing a vinaigrette where if there's too much oil, you add some vinegar, and if there's too much vinegar, you add some oil. It's that simple. You can use chiles fresh and unpeeled or you can smoke, roast, and then peel them.

Smoky flavor is an important note in Southwestern cooking. It is easy to cold-smoke peppers in a domed grill at low temperature (page 7). They acquire a wonderful smoky taste and can then be roasted.

It's a myth that the seeds carry all the heat in a chile pepper. In a chile just cut from the vine, the veins contain capsaicin, the heat-producing chemical, and the seeds have no heat at all. But as peppers age, the juice drips down from the veins to the seeds, making them heat carriers. I don't recommend seeding chiles unless you are going to stuff them, but since the seeds carry the heat in less fresh chiles, remove them if you prefer less heat. (Capsaicin is an irritant. If you have sensitive skin, wear rubber gloves when you work with chiles.) If you want a fresh chile at its hottest, leave the veins in. If you don't, cut the veins out. In a pepper that's been long off the vine, treat the seeds the same way.

In descending order of fire, here are the chiles I most often use.

Serrano

Narrow, about two inches long, it turns from green to red as it matures. It is very, very spicy, but it also has real pepper flavor, not just heat.

Jalapeño

Resembles a serrano but is larger and more tapered. It is about three inches long and half as wide, broader at the stem than at the base. It too ripens from green to red. The jalapeño is almost pure heat, but you can get more flavor by roasting it. I most often use it raw and very finely diced in salsas. It is available canned, but I strongly advise using fresh peppers.

Chipotle

A dried and smoky jalapeño, brownish in color, with a wrinkled skin and a fiery, smoky flavor. Chipotles are very versatile, and I use them to add an underlying note of smoky flavor to many dishes. Often I will make a sauce or vinaigrette, taste for seasoning, and find that it is missing something—and that's when I add chipotles. They are in my Roasted Vegetable–Green Chile Broth (page 82) and in the Red Chile Oil (page 127) that I brush on roasting chicken. Pureed and added to brioche (page 165), they give the bread a touch of spice and a beautiful orange-yellow color. If you use dried chipotles, you must rehydrate them before pureeing (page 8). Chipotles are also available canned in adobo sauce or red vinegar marinade. Puree them in a blender or food processor along with the sauce or marinade for the chipotle puree called for in recipes like Sweet Potato Soup with Smoked Chiles (page 20) or Corn and Wild Rice Pancakes (page 147).

Poblano

Resembles a green bell pepper but is pointy and very dark. It has thick flesh and a fresh pepper flavor. To me, this is the ultimate chile because it has such an incredible pepper flavor. It is roasted, skinned, seeded, and stuffed for chiles rellenos and roasted and added to sauces and salsas. Poblanos usually are not too hot, although they vary; in a box of 30 poblano peppers, you can get all kinds. They are supposed to have a little kick to them, but every once in a while people complain that they are too hot to eat.

Ancho

A dried poblano, red with a flavor almost like that of a slightly hot raisin. I rehydrate anchos and puree them into a paste for dark sauces like the Wild Mushroom–Ancho Chile Sauce (page 118). Anchos lend a sweet note, but they can be bitter; sometimes they have to be balanced with honey or maple syrup.

Anaheim

A long and thin, bright green, mild chile with very little heat. Roasted and sliced, it gives flavor to sautéed or roasted potatoes; roasted and diced, to sauces and salsas.

New Mexico red

A dried New Mexico green chile, similar to an Anaheim. It has a deep, roasted flavor and is not too spicy. Grind New Mexico reds for a pepper crust on steaks and fish steaks or rehydrate and puree them for dark sauces or stocks.

I also use **chile powders**. Prepared chile powders contain cumin, paprika, cayenne, and other additives. It is better to buy one kind of ground dried chile, such as pasilla or ancho chile powder.

Sweet Peppers

In addition to chile peppers, I use sweet peppers, particularly red, green, and yellow bell peppers. I always roast, smoke, or grill bell peppers; I make vinaigrettes, sauces, and oils with them.

Other Ingredients

Avocado

Haas avocados from California, which are smaller and have a more pronounced flavor than those from Florida, are preferable. They have a dark, pebbly skin and are slightly soft when ripe.

Banana leaves

Banana leaves, which are available fresh or frozen at Hispanic markets, are used to wrap fish or tamales. They impart a subtle flavor to the wrapped food, as in the Red Snapper Roasted in Banana Leaves with Red Curry Sauce (page 97). The leaves are large; cut them into usable pieces. You can store them in the freezer.

Butter, compound

Softened butter mixed with herbs or other flavorings (margarine is not an acceptable substitute). I melt compound butter over corn tamales, steak, and roasted corn on the cob.

Cilantro

Also known as coriander or Chinese parsley. Cilantro has a pungent odor and distinctive flavor. Use fresh cilantro only.

Chorizo

A spicy, garlic-flavored pork sausage available in Hispanic markets and many supermarkets.

Citrus

Grapefruit, oranges, and limes enhance and bring out the flavors of grilled fish. Also used in citrus vinaigrette.

Coconut milk, unsweetened

Used not to give coconut flavor but to counterbalance very strong flavors, like chiles or red curries. It is available canned.

ingredients, techniques & equipment

Corn

Served as a vegetable, roasted, grilled, or sautéed, on or off the cob. There is no substitute for fresh corn. In the colder months you can find corn from Texas or other Southern states in the market. By summer, it's easily available in the Northeast. One ear of corn yields about one-half to three-quarters of a cup of kernels.

Corn husks, dried

For wrapping tamales, they must first be soaked in water until they soften. Dried corn husks are available at Hispanic markets and many supermarkets.

Cornmeal

Available in fine, medium, and coarse grinds. Medium and coarse grinds are used to make muffins and breads; fine or medium grinds in batters and as breading. I use both yellow cornmeal, which is the most common and can be found in supermarkets, and blue cornmeal, which is available at specialty stores and by mail (page 205). Blue corn is organically grown; the meal has more flavor than the yellow. To make seasoned cornmeal (yellow or blue), add one tablespoon salt and one tablespoon freshly ground black pepper to each cup of cornmeal.

Crème fraîche

Slightly soured and thickened cream. It can be heated without curdling. You can buy it or make your own. To make crème fraîche, add two tablespoons buttermilk to one cup heavy cream, cover, and leave at room temperature until thickened, from 8 to 24 hours. Can be refrigerated for up to 10 days.

Cumin

A dried, aromatic seed. I use it toasted and ground.

Curry paste

Made from ground chile peppers, either red or green, and a mixture of spices. It is available in Asian markets or they can be ordered by mail (see Sources, page 205).

Curry Powder

4 tablespoons ancho chile powder
2 teaspoons cayenne
2 tablespoons ground cumin seed
2 tablespoons ground coriander seed
1 tablespoon ground fenugreek seed
2 teaspoons ground cardamom seed
4 tablespoons ground turmeric
2 teaspoons ground ginger
1 tablespoon freshly ground black pepper
1 tablespoon ground cloves

Combine the ingredients and store in tightly covered jar.

Makes about 1 cup

Flour, seasoned

To each cup of all-purpose flour add one tablespoon salt and one tablespoon freshly ground black pepper.

Garlic

Use minced raw garlic in salads, sautéed or roasted whole cloves in sauces and vinaigrettes.

Ginger

A spicy and slightly sweet root. Use it peeled and sliced or minced. Fresh and ground ginger are different and usually cannot be substituted for one another.

Herbs

I always use fresh herbs such as basil, oregano, and thyme, and I don't consider dried herbs a good substitute. To me, all dried herbs taste like tea, and I list them in my recipes only as a concession. If you must include dried herbs, use one-third the quantity of fresh.

Jícama

A sweet, crunchy root vegetable. Serve it peeled and raw in salads and relishes. It tastes like a combination of apple and potato.

Mango and papaya

Tropical fruits used in salsas, pretty much interchangeably. The mango has an oddly shaped pit that clings to the flesh, making the fruit difficult to slice (see below). The papaya, on the other hand, has small black seeds that are easy to scrape out.

Mesclun

A mixture of young greens for salad, available at many greengrocers.

Posole

Whole hominy (dried corn kernels) processed with lime and hulled. The kernels are puffy and have a bland flavor. Cooked posole is available canned at Hispanic markets.

Queso fresco

A soft white cheese made from cow's milk. Monterey Jack cheese can be substituted.

Texas caciotta cheese

A mozzarella-type cheese with red and green chile peppers, available by mail from The Mozzarella Company (page 205). Monterey Jack with jalapeños can be substituted.

Tomatoes

Use ripe fresh tomatoes whenever you can; canned tomatoes are for cooked sauces only. Red tomatoes have much more acidity than yellows. When you make a salsa with yellow tomatoes, use more lime juice or vinegar to add acidity.

Tortillas

Mexican flatbread made of wheat flour or blue, yellow, or white cornmeal. Both flour and cornmeal tortillas can be fried or steamed. Flour tortillas can also be baked (always on a dry pan) or grilled, but corn tortillas cannot because they become brittle.

Techniques

To blanch vegetables

Plunge vegetables into rapidly boiling water and cook until al dente. Then submerge them in ice water and drain.

To cold-smoke

Prepare a charcoal or wood fire in a domed grill and let it burn down to embers. Lay chips of soaked aromatic wood over the ashes—you just want to get the smoke going, not a very hot fire. (Food won't be cooked, but it will be infused with a smoky flavor.) Arrange the food on the grill rack. Open the top vent slightly and cover the grill so that the smoke stays inside. Smoke meats for about 15 minutes, and peeled, deveined shrimp for about 10 minutes per pound. Rub peppers with olive oil first and smoke for 20 minutes. Rub tomatoes with olive oil first and smoke for 10 minutes.

To cut mangoes

First, with a small, sharp knife, peel off the skin. Then cut down one side of the flesh, feeling your way along the pit with the knife; repeat on the opposite side. You will have two large pieces. Two smaller pieces of the fruit will remain, which you can cut off the same way. (You won't get four equal pieces, just two large and two smaller ones.)

To cut into chiffonnade

You don't want to chop basil or sage because chopping crushes the leaves. Instead, roll the leaves up tight and slice thin crosswise. The resulting strips are called chiffonnade.

To peel tomatoes

Plunge tomatoes into boiling water for several seconds, then into cold water. The skins slip off easily.

ingredients, techniques & equipment

To puree rehydrated ancho or other dried chiles

Drain well and process to a paste in a food processor. For more flavor, add some freshly chopped cilantro and garlic and process together with the chiles.

To rehydrate ancho or other dried chiles

Put the chiles in a mixing bowl, pour boiling water over them to cover, and let them sit for a couple of hours. When they are soft, remove the seeds and stems and drain the flesh.

Ancho Puree

6 anchos
8 cups boiling water
1 tablespoon minced garlic
2 tablespoons chopped fresh cilantro

Place the anchos in a bowl and pour the boiling water over them. Let stand for at least 30 minutes, or as long as overnight. Drain well, remove the seeds and stems, and place the flesh in a food processor with the garlic and cilantro. Process to a puree. *May be made up to 2 days ahead and refrigerated, covered.*
Makes 2 cups

To roast beets

Preheat the oven to 350° F. Wrap whole beets, all the same size, in foil, place them on a baking sheet, and roast for 45 minutes. Unwrap the beets and peel them.

To roast corn

Preheat the oven to 350° F. Prepare corn for roasting by removing all the silk and all but one layer of husk; dip each ear in water to moisten. Arrange the corn, husks covering kernels, on a baking sheet and roast for 45 minutes. Serve the ears whole or scrape the roasted kernels from the ears with a knife. One ear of corn will yield about one-half cup of kernels.

To roast garlic

Preheat the oven to 350° F. Rub individual garlic cloves with olive oil, place in a small ovenproof pan, and season with salt and pepper. Cover the pan with aluminum foil and roast for 45 minutes, or until garlic is soft and lightly browned. Peel the garlic.

To roast new potatoes

Preheat the oven to 350° F. Rub medium-size potatoes with olive oil, sprinkle with salt and pepper, and place on a baking sheet. Roast for 45 minutes.

To roast pearl onions

Preheat the oven to 350° F. Rub the onions with olive oil, sprinkle with salt and pepper, and place on a baking sheet. Roast for 45 minutes.

To roast peppers

Preheat the oven to 350° F. Rub peppers with olive oil, place on a baking sheet, and roast for 25 minutes. Remove from the oven and place in a brown paper bag for five minutes to steam. Cut the peppers in half, remove the stems and seeds, peel off the skin, and dice. For chiles rellenos, don't cut the poblanos in half; simply cut a slit down one side, remove the seeds, and peel the peppers.

To roast tomatillos

Preheat the oven to 400° F. Husk the tomatillos, rub with olive oil, and place on a baking sheet. Roast for 10 minutes.

To sweat vegetables

In a pan over medium or high heat, heat some oil and cook sliced vegetables slowly, stirring continually with a wooden spoon, until they soften without coloring.

ingredients, techniques & equipment

To toast cumin

Toast whole cumin seeds in a dry sauté pan over low heat for two to three minutes, tossing, until fragrant. You don't want them to color or burn.

To toast nuts

Preheat the oven to 350° F. Place the nuts on a baking sheet and toast for three to five minutes, taking care that they do not burn.

Equipment

Blender

The best tool for making vinaigrette and other emulsions is a blender. It has the power you need, and it doesn't incorporate as much air as a food processor does.

Cast-iron pans

For recipes in this book, you'll need a six-inch pan for cornbread and 10- and 12-inch sauté pans. They hold heat very well, they last forever, and they're cheap. Just don't use water on them. Scrub them with a steel pad and wipe them out.

Coffee grinder

Buy an inexpensive electric coffee grinder to use just to grind spices. Freshly ground spices are superior to anything you buy already ground, and you can control the coarseness.

Food processor

This is the essential tool for making compound butters, purees, and soups.

Grill

Any sturdy grill will do for cooking; a domed grill is needed for cold-smoking.

Hand-held blender

With a portable blender, puree soups and sauces right in the pot, rather than transferring them to a stationary blender or food processor.

Mandoline

A hand-operated slicer used for vegtables and other foods.

Juice extractor

Use for mangoes, papayas, carrots, and smoked yellow peppers.

Juicer

Use for fresh citrus.

Smoker

While there are excellent smokers available, you can cold-smoke food very easily in any domed grill.

Squeeze bottles

Squeeze bottles are imperative in your kitchen. They keep things neat and contained and give you control of your sauces. Refrigerate extra sauce in the squeeze bottles as well. (You can find small plastic squeeze bottles in beauticians' supply stores.)

ingredients, techniques & equipment

soups

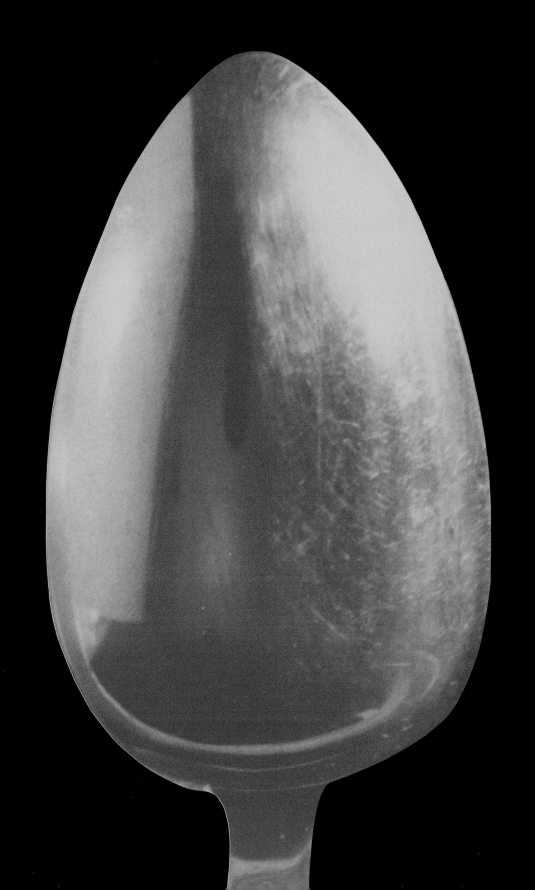

i didn't want to ruin the flavor

of those incredible tomatoes,

so i didn't put in anything that would get in

their way.

m ost of the soups I prepare are simple and based on vegetables, like White Bean and Roasted Tomato Soup with Sage Pesto, a garlicky, pink puree enlivened by chipotle; and Black Bean and Jalapeño Soup, a chunky winter kettle of beans and vegetables with warming chiles.

Some are not even made with stock. Tomato-Tortilla Soup is mainly fresh tomatoes—it works only when you have the best of the season. When I was first developing the recipe, I tried pouring some stock over the tomatoes and just letting them cook, but the soup turned out to be too watery. Then I decreased the amount of stock, but it was still too loose. What I wound up doing was just slowly cooking perfect, ripe tomatoes—nothing else—and then pureeing them, and that became the base. I didn't want to ruin the flavor of those incredible tomatoes, so I didn't put in anything that would get in their way. Once I had the base, I added some onions and garlic and white wine and reduced it, and then added a lot of fresh cilantro and a touch of cayenne. It's a very uncomplicated soup, with an intense tomato flavor and fantastic color.

Yellow Tomato Gazpacho is another soup with fervent tomato flavor, only this time the tomatoes are yellow, summer's sweetest. The soup is served cold, preferably as soon as you have mixed it, so that the tomatoes, peppers, and cucumbers remain crunchy and all the flavors stay sharp.

Thick Sweet Potato Soup with Smoked Chiles is almost a puree, and the rich flavor and texture of sweet potatoes are dominant. But each spoonful packs a surprise jolt of smoldering chipotles.

Posole traditionally is a poor man's dish, a long-cooked Mexican pork stew with tomatillos and hominy. My Shellfish Posole is quick, not something that cooks forever. Because the ingredients stew together in the broth so briefly, their flavors remain separate and intense.

Roasted Corn Soup with Smoked Chile Cream is the simplest of dishes, with an incredible corn flavor that comes from fresh-roasted corn. For its inspiration, I thank Florence Fabricant, the food writer, who let me in on the secret of roasting. She tasted my corn relish at the Miracle Grill and asked, "How did you cook the corn?" I told her I sautéed it, and she said, "No, don't do that—roast it." I tried her idea, and it worked. Roasted corn is truly delicious.

How can chowder, a chunky mix of potatoes and seafood that reminds everyone either of New England or Manhattan, be Southwestern? You have to taste my Curried Corn and Fresh Clam Chowder to understand. This recipe takes some time to prepare, but it's an amazing chowder, worth your effort.

Fish, lobster, and chicken stocks are the foundation of many of these soups and are useful in other recipes as well, so I include simple, basic recipes.

White Bean & Roasted Tomato Soup with Sage Pesto

Pureeing the red tomatoes with the white beans gives this soup a beautiful deep pink color. Since the tomatoes are roasted, "winter" tomatoes are acceptable here. When the tomatoes are roasted, their skins will blacken, but that black is absorbed in the puree. Full-flavored sage pesto adds the finishing green touch.

    3 large ripe tomatoes
    2 tablespoons unsalted butter
    1 medium onion, roughly chopped
    3 garlic cloves, roughly chopped
    1 cup dry white wine
    3 cups small navy beans, rinsed in
        cold water, picked over, and soaked in
        water to cover overnight
    4 cups Chicken Stock (page 16) or water
    1 tablespoon pureed canned chipotles
    2 tablespoons fresh lime juice
    Salt and freshly ground pepper
    Sage Pesto, to taste

1. Preheat the broiler or prepare a wood or charcoal fire. On an oiled rack, broil or roast the tomatoes for 10 minutes, turning, until the skins are blackened. Set aside.

2. In a saucepan over medium heat, melt the butter and sweat the onion and garlic for 5 minutes, or until translucent. Raise the heat to high, add the wine, and bring to a boil. Reduce for 10 to 15 minutes, or until the wine has completely evaporated.

3. Drain the beans. Reduce the heat to medium, add the beans and stock, and cook uncovered for 45 minutes to 1 hour, or until the beans are cooked through. Remove from the heat and add the pureed chipotles, lime juice, and salt and pepper to taste. Stir to combine. Remove half the mixture and puree in a food processor, then return it to the pot and stir well.

4. Break up the reserved tomatoes and add them to the soup. Remove half the mixture and puree in a food processor. Return it to the pot, reheat, and stir well. *May be made up to 2 days ahead, covered, and refrigerated.* Reheat, stirring, just before serving.

5. Serve hot in individual bowls, garnished with the pesto.

Makes 8 servings

Sage Pesto

Turning sage into pesto is a bit of a challenge. The emulsion doesn't hold together very well, so you have to stir it up just before you use it.

Besides the soup, sage pesto enhances strong-flavored fish like bass, swordfish, grouper, and tuna, as well as poultry.

    ½ cup sage leaves
    ½ cup parsley leaves
    2 garlic cloves
    3 tablespoons pine nuts
    2 tablespoons grated parmesan
    ½ cup olive oil
    Salt and freshly ground pepper

In a food processor, combine the sage, parsley, garlic, pine nuts, and cheese and process for 20 seconds, slowly adding the olive oil while the machine is running. Transfer to a mixing bowl and add salt and pepper to taste. *May be prepared up to 1 day ahead, covered, and refrigerated.* Bring to room temperature before serving.

Makes about 1 cup

Tomato Tortilla Soup

This is an uncomplicated soup, with intense tomato flavor and fantastic color. Any spices you add should just heat up the soup a little bit, they shouldn't get in the way of the tomatoes.

- 3 tablespoons unsalted butter
- 1 medium onion
- 2 garlic cloves, minced
- 2 cups dry white wine
- 10 very ripe tomatoes, cored and cut into thin wedges
- 2 cups chopped cilantro
- 1 tablespoon cayenne
- Salt and freshly ground pepper

GARNISH:
- 2 cups peanut oil
- Four 6-inch corn tortillas, preferably blue corn, cut into ½-inch-wide strips
- 2 Haas avocados, cut into ½-inch dice
- 2 cups grated white cheddar
- 24 cilantro sprigs, or to taste

1. In a saucepan over medium heat, melt the butter and sweat the onion and garlic for 5 minutes, or until translucent. Raise the heat to high, add the wine, and bring to a boil. Reduce for 10 to 15 minutes, or until the wine has completely evaporated.

2. Reduce the heat to low, add the tomatoes, and cook for 25 minutes, stirring occasionally. The tomatoes will be soupy but still chunky.

3. With a hand blender or in a food processor, puree the mixture until smooth. Add the cilantro, cayenne, and salt and pepper to taste and mix. *May be prepared up to 2 days ahead, covered, and refrigerated.* Reheat before serving. Dice the avocados and add them just before serving.

4. In a saucepan over medium heat, heat the peanut oil to 360° F., or until a tortilla strip sizzles when immersed. Fry the tortilla strips for about 45 seconds, drain on paper towels, and set aside.

5. Reheat if necessary and divide the soup among 8 bowls. Garnish each with 4 tortilla strips standing up in the center, a quarter of the avocado, ¼ cup grated cheese, and 3 cilantro sprigs. Serve hot.
Makes 8 servings

Yellow Tomato Gazpacho

Yellow tomatoes are so sweet, you feel you are eating a fruit. Since they have very little acid, you'll need to mix in some lime juice for this soup. (If you want to make it with red tomatoes instead, use only half the lime juice.) Don't let it sit for too long, because the flavors will intensify and the texture will change.

- 4 large yellow tomatoes, peeled, seeded, and diced
- 1 medium red bell pepper, seeded and diced
- 1 medium green bell pepper, seeded and diced
- 2 jalapeños, minced
- ½ cup chopped cilantro
- ½ cup fresh lime juice
- 2 cups canned tomato juice
- 2 medium cucumbers, peeled, seeded, and diced
- 3 garlic cloves
- 6 slices good-quality white bread, crusts left on
- Salt and freshly ground pepper
- Cilantro sprigs

1. In a mixing bowl, combine the tomatoes, bell peppers, jalapeños, cilantro, lime juice, tomato juice, and half the cucumbers. Set aside.

2. In a food processor, puree the remaining cucumbers with the garlic and white bread. Add to the tomato mixture, season with salt and pepper to taste, and refrigerate long enough to chill. *May be kept for 1 day, but no longer.* Best if served within a couple of hours of completion.

3. Serve cold, garnished with cilantro sprigs.
Makes 10 servings

Black Bean & Jalapeño Soup

Shiny black, thick, and stick-to-the-ribs, this is probably the best-known Southwestern soup. In the colder months of fall and winter, everyone appreciates its warmth and richness. This version omits the traditional pork, lightening the flavor and fat a little. You can use water in place of stock for a totally vegetarian dish.

2 tablespoons unsalted butter
1 medium carrot, scraped and
   coarsely chopped
1 medium onion, coarsely chopped
3 garlic cloves, roughly chopped
1 cup red wine
3 cups black turtle beans, rinsed in cold
   water and picked over
4 jalapeños, roasted, peeled,
   and seeded (page 8)
1 poblano, roasted, peeled, and seeded
   (page 8)
4 cups Chicken Stock or water
2 tablespoons fresh lime juice
Salt and freshly ground pepper
2 jalapeños, roasted (page 8)
   but not peeled or seeded, pureed in
   the blender
½ cup sour cream (optional)

1. In a saucepan over medium heat, melt the butter and sweat the carrot, onion, and garlic for 5 minutes, or until translucent. Add the wine, bring to a boil, and let reduce 10 to 15 minutes.

2. Drain the beans. Reduce the heat to medium, add the seeded jalapeños, poblano, beans, and stock, and simmer for 45 minutes to 1 hour, or until the beans are cooked through. Remove from the heat and add lime juice, and salt and pepper to taste. Stir to combine. Remove half the mixture and puree in a food processor, then return it to the pot and stir well. Reheat if necessary. *May be made up to 2 days ahead, covered, and refrigerated.* Reheat, stirring, just before serving.

3. Divide the soup among 8 bowls and garnish each with the pureed jalapeños and 1 tablespoon of sour cream, if desired.

Makes 8 servings

Chicken Stock

2 pounds chicken carcasses
2 medium celery stalks, coarsely chopped
2 medium carrots, coarsely chopped
1 medium onion
6 peppercorns
1 bay leaf
8 parsley sprigs

Combine all the ingredients in a large pot, add 8 cups cold water, and bring to a boil over high heat, skimming any scum that forms. Reduce the heat to low and simmer uncovered for 2 hours. Strain through cheesecloth or a fine strainer and degrease. Discard the solids. *May be covered and refrigerated for 2 days or frozen.*

Makes 8 cups

Fish Stock

3 pounds bones from snapper
   or any white fish
2 medium celery stalks, leaves removed,
   coarsely chopped
2 medium onions, coarsely chopped
½ cup black peppercorns
2 bay leaves
2 cups white wine

Combine all the ingredients in a large pot, add water to cover, and bring to a boil over high heat. Reduce the heat to low and simmer, uncovered, for 30 minutes. Strain and discard the solids. *May be covered and refrigerated for 2 days or frozen.*

Makes 4 to 8 cups

Lobster Stock

Next time you serve lobsters, save the shells for this stock.

2 tablespoons oil
Chopped shells of 2 roasted or
 boiled lobsters
1 large onion, chopped
1 small carrot, chopped
½ medium celery stalk, chopped
1 cup white wine
2 medium tomatoes, chopped,
 or ½ cup canned plum tomatoes
1 bay leaf
Salt

In a large saucepan over high heat, heat the oil and sauté the shells, onion, carrot, and celery for 5 minutes, stirring. Add the wine, tomatoes, bay leaf, salt, and 6 cups water. Reduce the heat to medium, partly cover, and simmer for 40 minutes. Strain and discard the solids. *May be covered and refrigerated for 2 days or frozen.*

Makes 4 to 5 cups

Shellfish Posole Stew

My interpretation of this Mexican stew, traditionally a peasant dish made with pork and green chiles, is built on a sweet-salty lobster stock seasoned with anchos, for dark color and thickness, and chipotles, for smoky heat. I add tiny clams, jumbo sea scallops, and shrimp, crisp sticks of zucchini and carrots, and large pearls of hominy. It isn't like a traditional stew, because each quickly cooked ingredient stands out from the others. This makes a complete meal with just a salad of crisp frisée.

2 tablespoons unsalted butter or olive oil
1 medium onion, chopped
4 cups Lobster Stock
2 tablespoons pureed canned chipotles
 (5 to 6 chiles)
2 tablespoons ancho puree (page 8)
½ cup honey
Salt and freshly ground pepper
1 cup olive oil
16 large shrimp, shelled and deveined
16 large sea scallops
3 medium carrots, scraped and cut into
 thin 2-inch sticks
2 medium zucchini, cut into thin
 2-inch sticks
2½ cups canned posole, rinsed and well
 drained (two 16-ounce cans—there will
 be a bit extra)
40 small clams, such as manila clams
 or cockles
24 cilantro sprigs, or to taste

1. In a saucepan over medium heat, melt the butter and sweat the onion for 5 minutes, or until translucent. Reduce the heat to medium, add the stock, and simmer for 30 minutes. Add the pureed chipotles, ancho puree, and honey and simmer uncovered for another 15 minutes. Season to taste with salt and pepper and set aside. *May be made up to 2 days ahead, covered, and refrigerated.* Reheat, stirring, just before serving.

2. In a large saucepan over high heat, heat the olive oil and sauté the shrimp and scallops for 3 minutes on one side. Turn them over, reduce the heat to medium, and add the reserved broth, the carrots, zucchini, posole, and clams. Simmer, covered, for 4 to 5 minutes, or until the clams open. Discard any that do not open. Correct the seasoning.

3. Divide among 8 bowls. Garnish each serving with cilantro sprigs.

Makes 8 servings

Roasted Corn Soup
with Smoked Chile Cream

You can make this soup all year round because corn isn't seasonal anymore. In the winter it comes from Texas or the Carolinas, and although it is more expensive then, it is always good.

When I made this soup at a cooking demonstration for De Gustibus at Macy's, some people were uncomfortable about all the cream. I told them the cream can be cut to ½ cup, which will cut the yield only by about 1 serving. The soup would still have plenty of body from the pureed corn.

> 6 ears corn, roasted (page 8)
> 2 tablespoons unsalted butter
> 1 medium onion, finely diced
> 1 tablespoon minced garlic
> 2 cups dry white wine

> 5 cups Chicken Stock (page 16) or water
> 2 cups heavy cream
> ½ cup Smoked Chile Cream
>   (recipe follows)

1. Scrape the kernels from each ear of corn with a sharp knife, breaking them up into single kernels, and set aside.

2. In a large saucepan over medium heat, melt the butter and sweat the onion and garlic for 3 to 5 minutes. Add the wine, raise the heat to high, and let the wine reduce 10 to 15 minutes, to about 4 tablespoons. Reduce the heat to low, add the roasted corn kernels, and sweat for 5 minutes.

3. Raise the heat to high, add the stock, and bring to a boil. Reduce the heat to medium and simmer, uncovered, for 20 minutes. Raise the heat to high again, add the cream, and bring to a boil. Cook, stirring occasionally, for 10 to 15 minutes, or until the soup has slightly thickened.

4. In a food processor, puree three-fourths of the soup, return it to the saucepan, and season to taste. *May be made up to 2 days ahead, covered, and refrigerated.* Reheat, stirring, just before serving.

5. Divide the soup among 12 bowls and garnish each with the chile cream just before serving.

Makes 12 servings

Smoked Chile Cream

½ cup sour cream
2 teaspoons pureed canned chipotles
1 teaspoon fresh lime juice
Salt and freshly ground pepper

Combine the sour cream, pureed chipotles, lime juice, and salt and pepper. Mix well and refrigerate, covered, for up to 1 day.

Makes about ½ cup

Curried Corn & Fresh Clam Chowder

This is possibly the most complicated recipe in the book, but you can prepare several things ahead of time and combine them later. The curry powder can be mixed ahead and stored in a tightly covered jar. (The recipe in the Ingredients section will make more than you need for the chowder, and the leftovers are very handy.) You can cook the fish stock up to two days before you need it and store it covered in the refrigerator. You can roast the potatoes and onions up to four hours early and refrigerate them. Then your last-minute cooking will be minimal. Is it rewarding? When you see the red-gold color of this chowder, inhale its perfume, and feel its remarkable flavors jumping around in your mouth, you'll know the answer. Serve some hot, buttery Chipotle Brioche (page 165) alongside.

½ cup heavy cream
4 tablespoons unsalted butter
½ cup chopped onion
1 medium green apple, sliced
1 tablespoon chopped garlic
½ cup Curry Powder (page 6)
2 cups fresh corn kernels
4 cups Fish Stock (page 16) or clam broth
4 new potatoes, roasted and quartered
   (page 8)
24 pearl onions, roasted and peeled
   (page 8)
40 small clams (manila clams or cockles)
   or 20 large clams (cherrystones)
Salt and freshly ground pepper
½ cup chopped cilantro
8 lime wedges

1. In a small saucepan over medium-high heat, bring the cream to a boil, then boil gently until reduced by three-fourths. Remove from the heat. In a medium saucepan over medium heat, melt 2 table-spoons of the butter, add the onion, apple, garlic, and curry powder, and sauté until the onion is translucent. Add the reduced cream and stir well.

2. In a medium saucepan over medium heat, melt the remaining butter and cook the corn until heated through. Raise the heat to high, add the soup base and stock, and bring to a boil. Add the potatoes, onions, and clams. Cover and cook until the clams have opened. Discard any that do not open. Season to taste with salt and pepper.

3. Divide the soup among 8 bowls and serve hot, garnished with the cilantro and lime.

Makes 8 servings

Opposite: Curried Corn & Fresh Clam Chowder, left,
   Roasted Corn Soup, right

Sweet Potato Soup
with Smoked Chiles & Blue & Gold Tortillas

People are always surprised by this thick, rich, and orange-gold soup—food writer Gael Greene has called it "pure beta-carotene." If you like, you can cut the amount of cream in half, but the consistency will change. The result will be good, but will be a different dish.

    2 tablespoons unsalted butter
    1 medium onion, coarsely cut
    2 garlic cloves
    3 medium sweet potatoes, peeled and quartered
    4 cups Chicken Stock (page 16) or water
    ½ cup plus 2 tablespoons honey
    ½ cup crème fraîche (page 6), or heavy cream
    2 tablespoons pureed canned chipotles
    Salt and freshly ground pepper
GARNISH:
    2 cups peanut oil
    Two 6-inch blue corn tortillas,
       cut into ½-inch squares
    Two 6-inch yellow corn tortillas, cut into ½-inch squares

1. In a large saucepan over medium heat, melt the butter and sweat the onion and garlic for 5 minutes, or until translucent. Raise the heat to high, add the sweet potatoes and stock, and bring to a boil. Lower the heat to medium and simmer for about 30 minutes.

2. Remove from the heat and add the honey, crème fraîche, pureed chipotles, and salt and pepper to taste. Puree in a food processor and set aside. *May be made up to 2 days ahead to this point and refrigerated.* Reheat before serving.

3. In a saucepan over medium heat, heat the peanut oil to 360° F. or until a tortilla square sizzles when immersed. Fry the tortilla squares for about 30 seconds, drain on paper towels, and set aside. *May be made up to 1 day ahead.*

4. Divide the soup among 8 bowls. Sprinkle each with a handful of tortilla squares and garnish the center of each with the flavored sour cream, to taste.
Serve warm.
    Makes 8 servings

tamales +

quesadillas

these combinations are classic — how can you go wrong?

do *you* want to make a t a m a l e

with

peanut butter

+

jelly

?

Go ahead ! somebody will eat it.

I love tamales, and so does everyone I serve them to. A traditional tamale is a plump little package of masa (a dense cornmeal dough made with lard) wrapped in a corn husk and steamed. If you had one in Mexico, it would be kind of heavy and dry, with some pork or shrimp cooked in the middle, and it would be served unadorned.

But tamales are a peasant dish without any rules, so anything goes. I cut out the lard and lighten the masa mixture by adding pureed kernels of corn, which gives the tamales a fresh taste and aroma. They are so fragrant and flavorful, you can just throw some butter on top and eat them plain. The corn makes all the difference—the minute you cut into the wrapping, its wonderful aroma surrounds you. And corn makes the masa filling very light, almost like a couscous.

After the tamales are steamed, open them up on individual plates. You can spoon some savory shrimp and roasted garlic sauce or some extravagant wild mushroom sauce with truffles over the top. Don't worry about the timing: You can keep the tamales hot in the oven until you're ready to serve them, or you can reheat them and spoon sauce over them at the last minute.

I make another kind of tamale and serve it a little differently. I mix some pumpkin puree or diced cooked sweet potatoes into the masa. When the tamale is done, you cut open the top, add a dab of spicy or sweet compound butter, and warm it briefly in the oven. Then eat it as you would a baked potato.

Traditionally, a quesadilla is a tortilla turnover. To make one, you spread some chiles or cheese on half of a tortilla, fold it over the filling, and fry the turnover.

In my cooking, however, I like to break a rule or two. My quesadillas aren't folded over. They are stacked—three layers of tortillas separated by filling, a sort of club quesadilla. I came up with the idea when I worked at the Miracle Grill, a tiny place in the East Village in Manhattan. It was an underdog restaurant, very inexpensive, catering to the prevailing neighborhood attitude that even if everything costs three dollars, the customers will tell you it's too much.

The bottom line was that I didn't want to waste even a single tortilla. I had decided to bake the quesadillas on a dry pan, even though the conventional method is frying, because I wanted to eliminate extra fat. I put one tortilla on a baking pan and I said to myself, "OK, now what happens if the tortilla sticks? The whole dish will be destroyed." I thought, "Let me add another layer. This way if the bottom sticks, I still have another whole layer of the quesadilla and I can still serve that. I can just scrap that first layer." That's how my club quesadilla was born.

Always sprinkle some grated melting cheese, like Monterey Jack, between the layers—just a small amount to hold the whole thing together. It's important to remember that you don't want to use a lot of filling or a lot of cheese. The quesadilla should be thin and crisp, with nothing running out along the edges.

Layering the quesadillas allows for a lot of flexibility: One mixture can be baked with the tortillas and another added as a topping.

The things you combine in your quesadilla should all work in unison. The best way to ensure that is to use foods that you've eaten together before: goat cheese, tomato, and basil; mozzarella and prosciutto; chicken, eggplant, and red onions; even smoked salmon and dill. These combinations are classic—how can you go wrong? Do you want to make a tamale with peanut butter and jelly? Go ahead! Somebody will eat it.

Basic Tamales

Making tamales is a kitchen skill that anyone can learn, so don't be afraid to try. You may never work as fast as my tamale cook, Fernando, who turns out 10 tamales for every one I make, but that really doesn't matter. You can still make them in reasonable time and with very little effort. I usually use dried corn husks to enclose the masa filling, but you can also use banana leaves.

24 dried corn husks
MASA:
  1½ cups fresh or frozen corn kernels,
    preferably fresh
  1 medium onion
  2 cups Chicken Stock (page 16) or water
  6 tablespoons unsalted butter
  6 tablespoons shortening
  1½ cups yellow cornmeal
  1½ teaspoons sugar
  Salt and freshly ground pepper

1. About 2 hours before you plan to form the tamales, clean the husks under running water. Soak them in warm water for 2 hours, or until softened.

2. Puree the corn, onion, and stock in a food processor. Transfer the mixture to a mixing bowl and cut in the butter and shortening. Using your fingers, mix in the cornmeal, sugar, and salt and pepper to taste until there are no visible lumps of fat. The mixture will be a lot looser than you think it should be, but when the tamales are steamed it will dry out.

3. Remove the corn husks from the water and set aside the best 20 husks. Drain and pat dry. Tear the remaining husks into 1-inch-wide strips to be used for tying. Lay 2 husks flat on a work surface with the tapered ends facing out and the broad bases overlapping by about 3 inches. Place about ⅓ cup of masa mixture in the center. Bring the long sides up over the masa, slightly overlapping, and pat down to

close. (If the masa drips out a little at the seam, that is no problem.) Tie each end of the bundle with a strip of corn husk, pushing the filling toward the middle as you tie. Trim the ends to about ½ inch beyond the tie. *Tamales can be assembled up to 1 hour ahead and refrigerated.* Once cooked, they can be refrigerated up to 6 hours and reheated in a 350° F. oven for 30 to 45 minutes.

3. Arrange the tamales in a single layer on a steaming rack, cover tightly with foil, and steam over boiling water for 45 minutes.
    Makes 10 tamales

Baked Sweet Potato Tamale

with Orange-Honey Butter

When you reduce fresh orange juice to a syrup, you are left with pure orange flavor, which intensifies the sweetness of this sweet potato tamale. Like the pumpkin tamales, these are an excellent fall side dish.

10 Basic Tamales
2 medium sweet potatoes, boiled, peeled,
  and diced (2 cups)
1 cup Orange-Honey Butter
  (recipe opposite)

1. Prepare the tamales through Step 2.

2. Preheat the oven to 350° F.

3. Add the sweet potatoes to the masa and combine well. Fill and tie the corn husks and steam the tamales for 45 minutes.

4. To serve, cut a slit on the top of each tamale and push the ends toward the middle to expose the masa. Top with 1 tablespoon of orange-honey butter at room temperature, place briefly in the oven to melt the butter, and serve.
    Makes 10 tamales
    Makes 10 side-dish servings

Orange-Honey Butter

1 cup fresh orange juice
2 tablespoons honey
8 tablespoons (1 stick) unsalted butter,
   at room temperature
Salt and freshly ground pepper

1. In a small saucepan over high heat, bring the orange juice to a boil and reduce to the consistency of honey. Set aside.

2. In a food processor, blend the orange syrup, honey, butter, and salt and pepper to taste until smooth. The mixture will be soft.

3. Place a sheet of parchment paper or wax paper on a work surface. Arrange the butter along a long side and form into a roll about 1 inch in diameter, leaving a 1-inch border of paper. Roll up the butter in the paper and refrigerate for at least 30 minutes. *May be refrigerated for up to 3 days or frozen.*
Makes 1 cup

Blue Corn Tamales with Basil Butter

Fresh basil enhances the deep corn flavor of blue cornmeal, making this a great summer dish.

8 tablespoons (1 stick) unsalted butter
4 tablespoons basil chiffonnade
Salt and freshly ground pepper to taste
10 Basic Tamales (page 26)

1. Combine the butter, basil, and salt and pepper to taste in a food processor and blend until smooth.

2. Place a sheet of parchment paper or wax paper on a work surface. Arrange the butter along one long side and form into a roll about 1 inch in diameter, leaving a 1-inch border of paper. Roll up the butter in the paper and refrigerate for at least 30 minutes. May be refrigerated for up to 3 days or frozen. Makes ¼ pound basil butter.

3. Follow the masa recipe in Basic Tamales, substituting blue cornmeal for the yellow. Fill and steam the corn husks as in the basic recipe.

4. To serve, cut a slit on top of each tamale and push both ends of the tamale toward the middle to expose the masa. Top with 1 tablespoon of basil butter, place briefly in the oven to melt the butter, and serve.
Makes 10 tamales

Shrimp Tamale
with Roasted Garlic Sauce

When someone says, "I don't know what to order—suggest something," I always recommend this dish as an appetizer. So far it has pleased everybody. If a customer doesn't like this one, I can't win.

¾ cup vegetable oil
40 medium shrimp, shelled and deveined (about 1¼ pounds)
2 cups fresh corn kernels
½ cup chopped cilantro
10 Basic Tamales (page 26)
2½ cups recipe Roasted Garlic Sauce

1. In a large skillet over high heat, heat the vegetable oil and sauté the shrimp for 1 minute on each side. Reduce the heat to medium, add the sauce, corn, and cilantro, and stir to combine. Season to taste with salt and pepper.

2. Arrange 1 tamale on each serving plate. Cut off 1 end of the corn just to open it up, so the masa flows out of the husk onto the plate. Spoon 4 shrimps and a generous portion of sauce over the tamale and serve.

Makes 10 tamales
Makes 10 first-course servings

[Shrimp Tamale with Roasted Garlic Sauce, opposite

Roasted Garlic Sauce

6 garlic cloves, roasted and peeled (page 8)
1 medium onion, finely diced
1 cup white wine
2 cups heavy cream
Salt and freshly ground pepper

In a medium saucepan over high heat, combine the garlic, onion, and white wine, bring to a boil, and reduce by three-fourths. Reduce the heat to medium, add the cream, and let simmer for 15 to 20 minutes. Season to taste with salt and pepper. Transfer to a food processor and puree. *May be prepared up to 2 days ahead, covered, and refrigerated.* Bring to room temperature before serving.
Makes about 2½ cups

Wild Mushroom Tamale
with or without Black Truffles

Some people put truffles in a dish and you can't even taste them, but when I use truffles, you know what you are eating. If you're just going to put a dusting of truffles in, it's more a gesture than a flavor, and that definitely is not my style. When I did this tamale for a New Year's Eve dinner, I stood there and shaved about a ton of truffles over the tamales. You have to take a little bit of a financial beating on this recipe, and you should plan to invest in a couple of truffles. Why not? It's only money! When you put that plate down, you really will hear people say, "My God, I can't believe this!" Even without truffles, there's lots of flavor in this dish, with three kinds of wild mushrooms and plenty of garlic.

½ cup olive oil
2 tablespoons minced garlic
¼ cup diced onion
1 cup white wine
6 cups sliced fresh shiitake, cremini,
   and portobello mushrooms, 2 cups each
   or any combination
2 cups heavy cream
3 tablespoons fresh thyme leaves
Salt and freshly ground pepper
10 Basic Tamales (page 26)
Fresh black truffles

1. In a saucepan over medium heat, heat the olive oil and sweat the garlic and onion for 2 minutes. Add the wine, raise the heat to high, and reduce for 10 minutes to about 2 tablespoons.

2. Lower the heat to medium, add the mushrooms, and cook for 5 to 7 minutes, or until softened. Raise the heat to high, add the cream, and bring it to a boil. Reduce the heat to medium and simmer the sauce for 15 minutes. Remove from the heat, add the thyme, and season to taste with salt and pepper.

3. Arrange 1 tamale on each serving plate. Cut off 1 end of the tamale to open it up, so the masa flows out of the husk onto the plate. Spoon a generous portion of sauce over the tamale. Shave some truffles over each tamale.

   Makes 10 tamales
   Makes 10 first-course servings

Pumpkin Tamales
with Spiced Butter

This recipe represents a different breed of tamale, served without sauce and generously topped with a compound butter that melts into the masa. Serve the tamales simply, the way you would a baked potato. These are good to serve in the fall, with pork chops or lamb chops.

    1 cup canned pumpkin puree
    ¼ cup honey
    2 tablespoons ground cinnamon
    1 tablespoon ground ginger
    1 tablespoon ground nutmeg
    Salt and freshly ground pepper
    ½ recipe Masa (page 26)
    24 dried corn husks, soaked in warm
        water for 2 hours
    10 tablespoons Spiced Butter

1. In a mixing bowl, combine the pumpkin puree, honey, cinnamon, ginger, nutmeg, and salt and pepper to taste. Set aside. Place the masa in a separate mixing bowl and add the pumpkin mixture, marbling it through the masa. Do not combine the 2 mixtures completely. Fill and tie the corn husks as directed on page 26. Steam the tamales until done, about 45 minutes.

2. Preheat the oven to 350° F.

3. To serve, cut a slit on the top of each tamale and push the ends toward the middle to expose the masa. Top with 1 tablespoon of spiced butter, place briefly in the oven to melt the butter, and serve.

Makes 10 tamales
Makes 10 side-dish servings

Pumpkin Tamale with Spiced Butter, Sweet Potato
Tamale with Orange Honey Butter, and Blue Corn Tamale
with Basil Butter, opposite

Spiced Butter

    8 tablespoons (1 stick) unsalted
        butter, at room temperature
    1 tablespoon ground cinnamon
    2 teaspoons ground nutmeg
    2 teaspoons ground ginger
    1 teaspoon ground cloves
    1 tablespoon honey
    Salt and freshly ground pepper

1. Combine all the ingredients in a food processor and blend until smooth.

2. Place a sheet of parchment paper or wax paper on a work surface. Arrange the butter along a long side and form into a roll about 1 inch in diameter, leaving a 1-inch border of paper. Roll up the butter in the paper and refrigerate for at least 30 minutes. *May be refrigerated for up to 3 days or frozen.*
Makes 1 cup

Spicy Chicken, Eggplant, & Grilled Red Onion Quesadilla

Quesadilla fillings should be thin, so pound the chicken and slice the vegetables no more than a quarter of an inch thick. Instead of the sour cream, you could garnish this quesadilla with Tomatillo Salsa (recipe opposite).

MARINADE :
½ cup Chicken Stock (page 16) or water
2 jalapeños, sliced
2 tablespoons chopped cilantro
2 tablespoons fresh lime juice
2 tablespoons olive oil

4 chicken tenderloins or
    8 ounces skinless and boneless
    chicken breast, pounded thin
4 crosswise slices red onion,
    ¼ inch thick
4 lengthwise slices eggplant, unpeeled,
    ¼ inch thick
Three 6-inch flour tortillas, or 8-inch
    tortillas cut to size
¼ cup grated Monterey Jack
¼ cup grated white cheddar
Salt and freshly ground pepper
3 tablespoons sour cream

1. In a blender or processor, combine the marinade ingredients and blend until smooth. Place the chicken in a nonreactive pan or bowl, pour the marinade over it, cover, and refrigerate for 4 hours.

2. Prepare a charcoal fire and let it burn down to embers, or preheat the broiler. Preheat the oven to 450° F.

3. Remove the chicken from the marinade and discard the marinade. Grill the chicken 2 to 3 minutes on each side, or until cooked through. Grill the onion slices 2 minutes on each side and the eggplant 1½ minutes on each side. Set aside.

4. Place 2 tortillas on an ungreased baking sheet. Spread half the cheeses, chicken, eggplant, and onion on each and season to taste with salt and pepper. Stack the 2 layers and cover with the remaining tortilla. *May be prepared ahead up to this point and refrigerated.* Bake for 8 to 12 minutes, or until the tortillas are slightly crisp and the cheese has melted.

5. Cut into quarters and serve hot, garnished with sour cream.

Makes 4 first-course servings

Chorizo & Goat Cheese Quesadilla with Tomatillo Salsa

This combination of tomatillos and chorizo, a spicy pork sausage popular in Southwest cooking, is surprisingly subtle.

Three 6-inch flour tortillas, or 8-inch
    tortillas cut to size
¼ cup crumbled domestic goat cheese
¼ cup grated Monterey Jack
4 ounces chorizo
Salt and freshly ground pepper
½ cup Tomatillo Salsa, or to taste
    (recipe opposite)

1. In a skillet over medium-high heat, cook the chorizo for 10 to 12 minutes. Peel and slice thin.

2. Preheat the oven to 450° F.

3. Place 2 tortillas on an ungreased baking sheet. Spread half the cheeses and chorizo on each and season to taste with salt and pepper. Stack the 2 layers and cover with the remaining tortilla. *May be prepared to this point up to 4 hours ahead, covered, and refrigerated.* Bake for 8 to 12 minutes, or until the tortillas are slightly crisp and the cheese has melted.

4. Cut into quarters and serve hot, garnished with tomatillo salsa. Serve extra salsa in a bowl in the center of the table.

Makes 4 first-course servings

Tomatillo Salsa

8 medium tomatillos, husked and
   coarsely chopped
1 tablespoon finely diced red onion
½ tablespoon minced jalapeño
2 tablespoons fresh lime juice
2 tablespoons coarsely chopped cilantro
1 tablespoon olive oil
1 teaspoon honey
Salt and freshly ground pepper

Combine the tomatillos, onion, jalapeño, lime juice, cilantro, olive oil, and honey in a bowl. Season to taste with salt and pepper. *Refrigerate, covered, for up to 1 day.* Bring to room temperature before serving.

Makes about 1½ cups

Goat Cheese Quesadilla

with Tomato & Basil Salsa

This quesadilla is very European in style. Goat cheese and basil make a light quesadilla that glistens with a salsa that repeats its summery flavor.

Three 6-inch flour tortillas,
   or 8-inch tortillas cut to size
¼ cup grated Monterey Jack
1½ cups crumbled goat cheese
2 tablespoons chopped red onion
½ cup basil chiffonnade
Salt and freshly ground pepper
½ cup Tomato and Basil Salsa,
   or to taste

1. Preheat the oven to 450° F.

2. Place 2 tortillas on an ungreased baking sheet. Sprinkle half the cheeses, onion, and basil on each and season to taste with salt and pepper. Stack the 2 layers and cover with the remaining tortilla. *May be prepared to this point up to 4 hours ahead and refrigerated, covered.* Bake for 8 to 12 minutes, or until the tortillas are slightly crisp and the cheese has melted.

3. Cut into quarters and serve hot, garnished with salsa. Serve any extra salsa in a bowl in the center of the table.

Makes 4 first-course servings

Tomato & Basil Salsa

1 medium tomato, coarsely chopped
1 tablespoon finely diced red onion
1½ teaspoons minced seeded jalapeño
2 tablespoons balsamic vinegar
¼ cup fresh basil chiffonnade
1½ teaspoons olive oil
Salt and freshly ground pepper to taste

Combine the tomato, onion, jalapeño, vinegar, basil, and olive oil. Add salt and pepper to taste. *Cover and refrigerate for up to 1 day.* Bring to room temperature before serving. Serve any extra salsa in a bowl in the center of the table.

Makes about 1½ cups

Smoked Salmon & Dill Quesadilla
with Salmon Caviar

Here is an example of my maxim, "If it works, it will work as a quesadilla." Red onion, green dill, smoky salmon, and briny salmon caviar combine happily. Surprisingly, they also harmonize with Monterey Jack and cheddar cheese. Garnish with some refreshing dill sour cream.

**Three 6-inch tortillas, or 8-inch
 tortillas cut to size
¼ cup grated Monterey Jack
¼ cup grated white cheddar
2 tablespoons chopped red onion
2 tablespoons chopped dill
Salt and freshly ground pepper
4 thin slices smoked salmon
2 teaspoons salmon caviar
½ cup Dill Sour Cream**

1. Preheat the oven to 450° F.

2. Place 2 tortillas on an ungreased baking sheet. Sprinkle half the cheeses, onion, and dill on each and season to taste with salt and pepper. Stack the 2 layers and cover with the remaining tortilla. *May be prepared to this point up to 4 hours ahead and refrigerated, covered.* Bake for 8 to 12 minutes, or until the tortillas are slightly crisp and the cheese has melted. Cut into quarters and serve hot, garnished with smoked salmon, salmon caviar, and dill sour cream. Serve extra sour cream in a bowl in the center of the table.

Makes 4 first-course servings

Smoked Salmon and Dill Quesadilla with
Salmon Caviar, opposite

Dill Sour Cream

**½ cup sour cream, regular or low-fat
2 tablespoons chopped dill
Salt and freshly ground pepper**

 Combine the sour cream and dill and season to taste with salt and pepper. Cover and refrigerate. Bring to room temperature before serving. *May be prepared 2 days ahead and refrigerated, covered.*
Makes about ½ cup

Mozzarella, Prosciutto, & Fresh Thyme Quesadilla
with Tomato Relish

Quesadillas work well with ingredients from all cuisines. This one shows an Italian influence, but when you come right down to it, if you put mozzarella and proscuitto between tortillas, the finished dish is Southwestern.

**Three 6-inch flour tortillas, or 8-inch
 tortillas cut to size
4 thin slices fresh mozzarella
4 paper-thin slices prosciutto
2 tablespoons coarsely chopped
 fresh thyme leaves, or 2 teaspoons dried
Salt and freshly ground pepper
¼ cup Tomato Relish, or to taste (page 99)**

1. Preheat the oven to 450° F.

2. Place 2 tortillas on an ungreased baking sheet. Spread half the mozzarella, prosciutto, and thyme on each and season to taste with salt and pepper. Stack the 2 layers and cover with the remaining tortilla. *May be prepared to this point up to 4 hours ahead, covered, and refrigerated.* Bake for 8 to 12 minutes, or until the tortillas are slightly crisp and the cheese has melted.

4. Cut into quarters and serve hot, garnished with the relish.

Serves 4 as an appetizer

Barbecued Duck & Wild Mushroom Quesadilla with Spicy Mango Salsa

Preparation of this quesadilla is longer than for others, but you can do the duck, the sauce, and the salsa ahead of time and put them together shortly before serving.

1 cup New Mexico–style Barbecue Sauce
2 duck legs, skin removed
½ cup Chicken Stock (page 16) or water
3 tablespoons olive oil
½ cup sliced shiitake mushroom caps
Three 6-inch flour tortillas, or 8-inch
   tortillas cut to size
¼ cup grated Monterey Jack
¼ cup grated white cheddar
Salt and freshly ground pepper
1 teaspoon ancho chile powder
½ cup Spicy Mango Salsa, or to
   taste (recipe opposite)

1. Preheat the oven to 300° F.

2. Brush the barbecue sauce on the duck legs, place them in a casserole, and pour the stock around them. Cover and bake for 3 hours, basting with the barbecue sauce every 30 minutes. Allow to cool at room temperature. When the duck is cool enough to handle, pick the meat off the bones and set aside. *May be prepared up to 1 day ahead, covered, and refrigerated.* Reheat in a 350° F. oven for 15 minutes.

3. In a saucepan over medium heat, heat 2 tablespoons of the olive oil and sauté the mushrooms for 2 minutes, or until tender.

4. Preheat the oven to 450° F. Place 2 tortillas on an ungreased baking sheet. Spread half the cheeses, duck, and mushrooms on each and season to taste with salt and pepper. Stack the 2 layers, cover with the remaining tortilla, brush with 1 tablespoon oil, and sprinkle evenly with chile powder. *May be prepared ahead up to this point and refrigerated.*

Bake for 8 to 12 minutes, or until the tortillas are slightly crisp and the cheese has melted.

5. Cut into quarters and serve hot, garnished with the salsa.

Makes 4 first-course servings

New Mexico–Style Barbecue Sauce

You'll find you'll use this sauce a lot. It's the basis for the Peanut-Chipotle Sauce for barbecued ribs (page 122). It's also used to marinate salmon in New Mexico-style Barbecued Salmon (page 89) and with duck on page 136.

2 tablespoons unsalted butter
½ medium red onion, finely diced
1 garlic clove, finely diced
6 plum tomatoes, coarsely diced
¼ cup tomato ketchup
2 tablespoons Dijon mustard
2 tablespoons dark brown sugar
1 tablespoon honey
1 teaspoon cayenne
1 tablespoon ancho chile powder
1 teaspoon pasilla chile powder
1 tablespoon paprika
1 tablespoon Worcestershire sauce

1. In a large saucepan over medium heat, heat the butter and sweat the onion and garlic until translucent. Add the tomatoes and simmer for 15 minutes. Add the remaining ingredients and simmer for 20 minutes.

2. Puree the mixture in a food processor, pour into a bowl, and allow to cool at room temperature. *Will keep for 1 week refrigerated or several months frozen.*

Makes 5 cups

Spicy Mango Salsa

½ cup coarsely chopped mango
2 tablespoons finely diced red onion
1 teaspoon finely diced jalapeño
2 tablespoons coarsely chopped cilantro
3 tablespoons fresh lime juice
Salt and freshly ground pepper

Combine the mango, onion, jalapeño, cilantro, and lime juice. Season to taste with salt and pepper. Cover and set aside. *May be prepared up to 1 day in advance, covered, and refrigerated.* Bring to room temperature before serving.

Makes about 1 cup

Shrimp & Cilantro Pesto Quesadilla

Cilantro adds its sharp green presence to this quesadilla, which is topped with a sprinkling of brassy ancho chile powder.

4 large shrimp, shelled and deveined
Salt and freshly ground pepper
3 tablespoons olive oil
Three 6-inch flour tortillas or 8-inch
  tortillas cut to size
¼ cup grated Monterey Jack
¼ cup grated white cheddar
3 tablespoons Cilantro Pesto
  (page 77)
1 teaspoon ancho chile powder
2 teaspoons sour cream, or to taste

1. Preheat the oven to 450° F.

2. Season the shrimp with salt and pepper to taste. In a small skillet over medium heat, heat 2 tablespoons of the olive oil and sauté the shrimp 1½ minutes on each side. Reserve for garnish.

3. Place 2 tortillas on an ungreased baking sheet, sprinkle half the cheeses and 1½ tablespoons pesto on each, and season to taste with salt and pepper. Stack the 2 layers and cover with the remaining tortilla. Brush with 1 tablespoon oil and sprinkle evenly with ancho chile powder. *May be prepared 1 day ahead up to this point and refrigerated.* Bake for 8 to 12 minutes or until the tortillas are slightly crisp and the cheese has melted.

4. Cut into quarters and serve hot, garnished with the shrimp, more pesto, and sour cream.

Makes 4 first-course servings

Corn & Zucchini Quesadilla

with Smoked Tomato Salsa & Avocado Relish

This corn and zucchini quesadilla was the first quesadilla I ever made, years ago, and it has been the most popular item on the menu at the restaurant ever since.

What makes it so good? The flavors of fresh corn, crisp zucchini, and tangy cheeses work perfectly together. It is vegetarian, so anyone can enjoy it. With smoked tomato salsa and avocado relish, it is an elegant dish.

Three 6-inch flour tortillas, or 8-inch
  tortillas cut to size
¼ cup grated Monterey Jack
¼ cup grated white cheddar
2 tablespoons chopped red onion
1 jalapeño, minced
¼ cup julienned zucchini
¼ cup fresh corn kernels
Salt and freshly ground pepper
½ cup Smoked Tomato Salsa, or
  to taste
½ cup Avocado Relish, or to taste

1. Preheat the oven to 450° F.

2. Place 2 tortillas on an ungreased baking sheet. Spread half the cheeses, onion, jalapeño, julienned zucchini, and corn on each and season to taste with salt and pepper. Stack the 2 layers and cover with the remaining tortilla. *May be prepared ahead up to this point and refrigerated.* Bake for 8 to 12 minutes, or until the tortillas are slightly crisp and the cheese has melted.

3. Cut into quarters and serve hot garnished with the salsa and relish.

Makes 4 first-course servings

Smoked Tomato Salsa

2 medium cold-smoked tomatoes (page 7),
  seeded and coarsely chopped
2 tablespoons finely diced red onion
1 tablespoon minced jalapeño
¼ cup fresh lime juice
1 tablespoon ancho chile powder
  or good-quality prepared chile powder

Combine all the ingredients, cover, and refrigerate. Bring to room temperature before serving. Serve extra salsa in a bowl in the center of the table.
Makes about 2½ cups

Avocado Relish

1 ripe Haas avocado, coarsely chopped
1 tablespoon finely diced red onion
1 tablespoon minced jalapeño
2 tablespoons fresh lime juice
1 tablespoon coarsely chopped cilantro
Salt and freshly ground pepper

Combine the avocado, onion, jalapeño, lime juice, and cilantro. Season to taste with salt and pepper. *Cover and refrigerate for up to 1 day.* Bring to room temperature before serving. Place any extra in a bowl in the center of the table.
Makes about 1 cup

salads

+

salad dressings

sometimes it is hard to get people to see things in different ways,

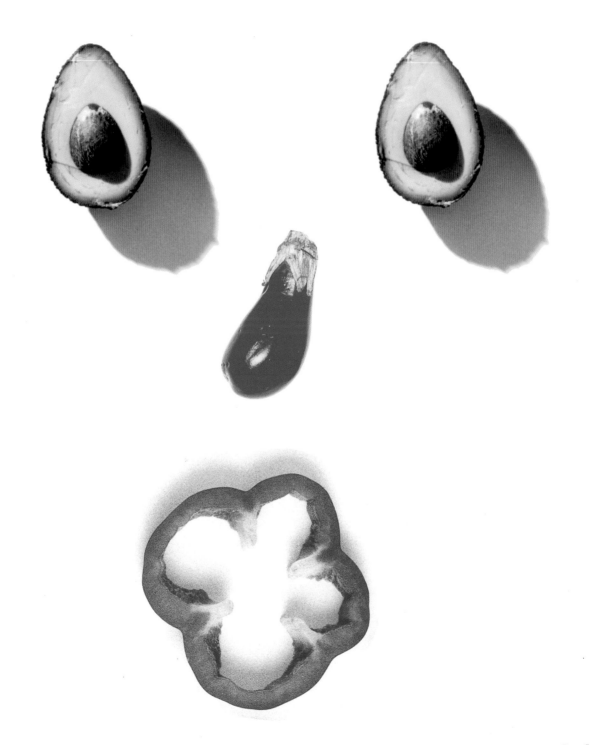

41

especially

things they are used to, like

s a l a d s

Sometimes it's hard to get people to see things in different ways, especially things they are used to, like salads. Once when I was a guest on the "Regis and Kathy Lee" television show, I made my Southwestern Potato Salad. It shocked Regis Philbin. "Are you really putting all that cilantro in there?" he wanted to know. "All of it," I assured him. (There wasn't really that much, just enough to overturn the traditional idea about potato salad.)

Salads are more than just an adjunct to the main course. Any one in this chapter, from the Caesar Salad with Red Chile Croutons to the hefty Pan-seared Snapper Salad with Warm Oregano Dressing, can be a meal in itself. If you want to use one of these salads as an accompaniment, my advice is to pair it with a quesadilla. Try the White Chicory Salad with Chorizo, Tomatoes, and Asiago Cheese with the Spicy Chicken, Eggplant, and Grilled Red Onion Quesadilla (page 32); the mixed Tomato and Mozzarella Salad with the Shrimp and Cilantro Pesto Quesadilla (page 37); or the Blue Corn–Fried Chicken Salad with a Corn and Zucchini Quesadilla (page 38). Combinations like these will increase the range of lively flavors and textures in each meal.

In many salads, I like to throw warm and cold ingredients together in unexpected ways. In my Red Chile–crusted Sea Scallops Salad, peppery salad greens play off sizzling seared scallops. In my Southwestern Tuna Salad, grilled tuna and potatoes contrast with crisp, cold greens, all dressed with a lively Basil-Garlic Vinaigrette. In Blue Corn–Fried Chicken Salad, slices of hot breaded chicken slightly wilt the crisp greens when they make contact. In the Grilled Shrimp Salad, two basic foods of summer, shrimp and corn, bounce off fresh thyme.

Another element in my salads is abundance. In the summertime, I like to make a Mixed Tomato and Mozzarella Salad using four or five different kinds of tomatoes. Use whatever you can get, as long as they are perfect. To add surprise, dress the salad with a Cilantro Vinaigrette. For another bounteous dish, I heap a multicolored assortment of grilled vegetables on crisp greens, dress the salad with balsamic vinaigrette, and garnish it with Goat Cheese Croutons (page 55).

When you buy salad ingredients, you'll find so many salad greens available that you can pick and choose the ones that look most appealing. Romaine, baby red, and mesclun are the tenderest lettuces. I really love peppery greens, like frisée and mizuna, for the sharp note they add.

It's a good idea to plan your salad first and then decide on the vinaigrette, so you can match them. Vinaigrettes are easy. You can make any herbed vinaigrette—basil, cilantro, thyme, oregano—simply by mixing oil, vinegar, and herbs. Use the ones I suggest or substitute others that appeal to you; they will make your salads bold. Although purists may not approve, I mix vinaigrettes in a blender and get perfect emulsions. (You could use a food processor, but I think it incorporates too much air.) Finally, I use a squeeze bottle, for both serving and storage. It gives excellent control in dressing the salads.

salads & salad dressings

Grilled Shrimp Salad

with Fresh Thyme Vinaigrette & Spicy Corn Relish

Shrimp and corn, two favorite summer foods, meet in this sunny salad. They are given a little jolt from the jalapeño and cilantro in the relish and the ancho chiles in the vinaigrette.

    16 large shrimp, peeled and deveined
    Olive oil
    Salt and freshly ground pepper
    4 cups mesclun or mixed red and
        green lettuce leaves
    ½ cup Thyme Vinaigrette
    6 tablespoons Corn Relish (page 103)

1. Prepare a charcoal or wood fire and let it burn down to embers, or preheat the broiler. Brush the shrimp with olive oil, season to taste with salt and pepper, and grill until just cooked, about 2½ minutes on each side. Set aside.

2. Dress the greens with about half of the vinaigrette and divide among 4 plates. Top each serving with 4 grilled shrimp and 1½ tablespoons of the relish. Drizzle vinaigrette over each portion to taste and serve.

    Makes 4 first-course servings

Thyme Vinaigrette

Be sure to use fresh thyme here; dried thyme simply will not work.
¼ cup fresh thyme leaves
3 tablespoons fresh lime juice
1 tablespoon finely diced red onion
1 teaspoon finely minced garlic
1 teaspoon ancho chile powder
½ cup olive oil
Salt and freshly ground pepper

   In a mixing bowl, combine the thyme, lime juice, onion, garlic, and chile powder. Slowly whisk in the oil and season to taste with the salt and pepper. *May be prepared up to 1 day ahead and refrigerated in a squeeze bottle.* Bring to room temperature before serving.
Makes about 1 cup

Mixed Tomato & Mozzarella Salad

with Cilantro Vinaigrette

Here is a beautiful salad to put out at a party for people to admire and enjoy, or to serve as a first course for a summer dinner. The colors of perfect summer tomatoes and greens against the creamy white mozzarella are enticing. If you can't find all these tomatoes at your market, get as many different kinds as possible.

1 large yellow beefsteak tomato,
 sliced ¾ inch thick
2 large red beefsteak tomatoes,
 sliced ¾ inch thick
8 yellow cherry tomatoes
8 red cherry tomatoes
8 yellow pear tomatoes
8 red pear tomatoes
1 pound fresh mozzarella,
 sliced ¾ inch thick
2 cups watercress or mizuna
1 cup Cilantro Vinaigrette

Divide the tomatoes equally among 4 plates and top each portion with a fourth of the mozzarella. Dress the watercress with 4 tablespoons cilantro vinaigrette and arrange it over the tomatoes. Drizzle each salad with vinaigrette to taste.

Makes 4 first-course servings

Cilantro Vinaigrette

2 cups (tightly packed) cilantro leaves
2 tablespoons red wine vinegar
1 tablespoon fresh lime juice
1 tablespoon minced garlic
1 tablespoon finely chopped red onion
1 tablespoon honey
½ cup olive oil
Salt and freshly ground pepper

Combine the cilantro leaves, vinegar, lime juice, garlic, onion, and honey in a blender and puree. With the motor running, slowly add the oil until emulsified. Season to taste with salt and pepper and pour into a squeeze bottle. *May be prepared up to 1 day ahead and refrigerated.* Bring to room temperature before serving

Makes about 1 cup

Southwestern Potato Salad

This summer salad became a Mesa Grill phenomenon after I prepared it on television. Guests request it all the time. It's one of the classics, an American favorite with a Southwestern twist.

1 cup good-quality prepared mayonnaise,
 regular or reduced-calorie
¼ cup Dijon mustard
2 tablespoons fresh lime juice
1 medium tomato, chopped
2 tablespoons chopped cilantro
½ jalapeño, finely diced
2 scallions, chopped, white and green parts
½ medium red onion, thinly sliced
½ teaspoon cayenne
1 small garlic clove, minced
Salt and freshly ground pepper
16 new potatoes, about 2 pounds, cooked,
 drained, and sliced ½ inch thick

With a spatula, combine the mayonnaise and mustard with the remaining ingredients, except the potatoes, and mix well. Season to taste and pour over the warm potatoes.

Makes 6 servings

Southwestern Grilled Tuna Salad

with Basil-Garlic Vinaigrette

This is my version of a Niçoise salad, given a Southwestern touch by the grilled tuna and the avocados.

4 tuna steaks (about 5 ounces each)
5 teaspoons olive oil
Salt and freshly ground pepper
4 new potatoes, cooked and slightly cooled
4 cups mesclun or mixed red and
   green lettuce leaves
½ cup Basil-Garlic Vinaigrette,
   or to taste
2 Haas avocados, peeled and sliced thin
2 medium tomatoes, cut into quarters
2 tablespoons Niçoise olives, pitted
2 tablespoons capers, drained

1. Prepare a wood or charcoal fire and let it burn down to embers, or preheat the broiler. Brush the tuna steaks with 4 teaspoons of the oil, season to taste with salt and pepper, and grill to desired doneness, 2 minutes for rare, 3½ minutes for medium, and 5 minutes for well done, turning once.

2. Brush the potatoes with 1 teaspoon of oil, grill and about 2 minutes, turning. When done, slice thick.

3. Dress the greens with about half of the vinaigrette and toss gently with the avocados, tomatoes, olives, and potatoes.

4. For each serving, place 1 tuna steak on a large plate and drizzle with a little vinaigrette. Arrange the salad around the tuna, giving each plate an equal portion of avocados, tomatoes, potatoes, and olives. Sprinkle with capers and serve.

Makes 4 main-course servings

Basil-Garlic Vinaigrette

2 cups (tightly packed) basil leaves
2 teaspoons red wine vinegar
1 tablespoon fresh lime juice
1 tablespoon minced garlic
1 tablespoon chopped red onion
1 tablespoon honey
½ cup olive oil
Salt and freshly ground pepper

   Combine the basil leaves, vinegar, lime juice, garlic, onion, and honey in a blender and puree. With the motor running, slowly add the oil until emulsified. Season to taste with salt and pepper and pour into a squeeze bottle. *May be prepared up to 1 day ahead and refrigerated.* Bring to room temperature before serving.

Makes about 1 cup

Blue Corn–Fried Chicken Salad

with Cayenne-Buttermilk Dressing

salads & salad dressings

Take some crisp fried chicken (dark meat works best), crunchy on the outside and moist on the inside. Then build a salad around it, with roasted red and yellow bell peppers, roasted beets, and crisp greens, and top it all with a spicy ranch-style dressing. See page 8 for how to roast the vegetables. I prefer to bread the chicken with blue cornmeal, but you can substitute the yellow, if necessary.

2 large eggs, lightly beaten
1 tablespoon Worcestershire sauce
1 tablespoon Tabasco sauce
Salt and freshly ground pepper
1 cup seasoned blue cornmeal (page 6)
4 skinless and boneless chicken thighs
2 cups peanut oil
4 cups mesclun or mixed red and
     green lettuce leaves
2 medium red bell peppers, roasted,
     peeled, seeded, and julienned
2 medium yellow bell peppers, roasted,
     peeled, seeded, and julienned
2 medium beets, roasted, peeled,
     and sliced
4 tablespoons Balsamic Vinaigrette
     (page 55)
¾ cup Cayenne-Buttermilk Dressing

1. In a mixing bowl, combine the eggs, Worcestershire sauce, Tabasco sauce, and salt and pepper to taste. Pour the cornmeal into a shallow bowl. Dip the chicken into the egg mixture and dredge with cornmeal.

2. Heat the oil to 375° F., or until edge of meat sizzles when immersed, and fry the chicken for about 5 minutes, turning until brown on all sides. *May be prepared several hours ahead, covered, and refrigerated.*

3. Dress the mesclun with the vinaigrette and arrange on the top halves of 4 plates. Slice the chicken 1 inch thick and arrange each thigh in a fan shape beneath the greens. Scatter the peppers and beets over the chicken and dress generously with the cayenne-buttermilk dressing.
    Makes 4 main-course servings

Cayenne-Buttermilk Dressing

2 tablespoons sour cream,
     regular or low-fat
½ cup buttermilk
1 teaspoon minced garlic
1 teaspoon minced red onion
1 tablespoon fresh lime juice
½ t. ~~1 teaspoon cayenne~~ *teaspoon*
Salt and freshly ground pepper

    Combine the sour cream, buttermilk, garlic, onion, lime juice, and cayenne. Add salt and pepper to taste. Mix well. *May be prepared 1 day ahead and refrigerated in a squeeze bottle.*
    Makes ½ cup

White Chicory Salad

with Chorizo, Tomatoes, Asiago Cheese, & Roasted Garlic Vinaigrette

I always have loved the French country salad that combines chicory, bacon, Roquefort cheese, and roasted garlic cloves, and this is my Southwestern version. I substitute white chicory (frisée) for the green; chorizo sausage for the bacon; and asiago cheese for the Roquefort. I add cilantro and puree the roasted garlic into a silky vinaigrette. It's still a country salad, but I've changed the country.

½ pound chorizo sausage, sliced
  ⅛ inch thick
4 cups white chicory or curly endive
1 cup Roasted Garlic Vinaigrette
2 medium tomatoes, cut into eighths
¼ pound asiago cheese, finely shaved,
  or young parmesan
½ cup chopped cilantro

1. In a skillet over low heat, cook the sausage for 10 minutes to render fat. Remove from the pan, drain on paper towels, and set aside.

2. Dress the chicory with 4 tablespoons of the vinaigrette and divide among 4 plates. Dress the tomatoes with 2 tablespoons vinaigrette and divide among the 4 plates. Sprinkle the top and edges of the salad with the chorizo, cheese, and chopped cilantro.

Makes 4 main-course servings

Roasted Garlic Vinaigrette

8 garlic cloves, roasted and peeled (page 8)
2 tablespoons red wine vinegar
1 tablespoon chopped red onion
1 tablespoon honey
1 tablespoon fresh lime juice
½ cup olive oil
Salt and freshly ground pepper

Combine the garlic, vinegar, onion, honey, and lime juice in a blender and puree. With the motor running, slowly add the oil until emulsified. Season to taste with salt and pepper. Pour into a squeeze bottle. *May be prepared up to 1 day ahead and refrigerated.* Bring to room temperature before serving.

Makes about 1 cup

Caesar Salad

with Red Chile Croutons

In this Southwestern version of a Caesar Salad, ancho chile powder heats up the croutons and pureed chipotles enliven the dressing. There is no raw egg in this dressing.

4 cups green romaine lettuce, inner
    leaves only
½ cup Spicy Caesar Dressing
Red Chile Croutons
¼ cup grated parmesan
12 leaves red romaine lettuce, if available
12 anchovy fillets

1. Place the green romaine in a large bowl, add the dressing, croutons, and half the parmesan, and toss together.

2. Divide the salad among 4 individual bowls, sprinkle with the remaining parmesan, and arrange the red romaine leaves, if available, in the center of each serving. Sprinkle the anchovies around the edge of the salad.

Makes 4 first-course servings

Red Chile Croutons

8 slices French or Italian bread, ½ inch thick
¼ cup olive oil
1 teaspoon ancho chile powder
Salt and freshly ground pepper to taste

Preheat the oven to 350° F. Toss the bread with the olive oil and place on a baking sheet. Sprinkle with the chile powder and salt and pepper to taste. Bake for about 7 minutes, or until lightly browned.

Makes 4 servings

Spicy Caesar Dressing

1 tablespoon prepared mayonnaise
1 teaspoon Dijon mustard
1 teaspoon freshly ground pepper
1 teaspoon pureed canned chipotles
1 teaspoon Worcestershire sauce
Few drops Tabasco sauce
1 tablespoon fresh lime juice
1 teaspoon capers
10 anchovy fillets
8 garlic cloves, roasted or lightly
    sautéed (page 8)
1½ cups olive oil
1 tablespoon red wine vinegar

1. Put all the ingredients, except the oil and vinegar, in a food processor and process until coarsely blended. Transfer to a mixing bowl.

2. Slowly mix in the oil, then mix in the vinegar. If the dressing is very thick, mix in a little water. *May be prepared up to 1 day ahead and refrigerated in a squeeze bottle.* Bring to room temperature before serving.

Makes about 2 cups

Red Chile–crusted Sea Scallops

with Mango & Tortilla Salad & Orange Vinaigrette

The spice mixture for coating the scallops can be prepared up to one week ahead, but for a crispy crust don't dip the scallops into it until the last second before frying. If you want to skip the step of reducing the orange juice for the vinaigrette, substitute three tablespoons of undiluted frozen orange juice for the reduced fresh juice.

The salad greens should be very lightly dressed by the orange vinaigrette. Place the greens in a deep bowl and spoon the vinaigrette around the sides of the bowl or squirt it from a squeeze bottle and move the leaves up into the dressing and back down.

3 tablespoons ancho chile powder
2 tablespoons ground toasted
   cumin (page 9)
1 teaspoon salt
1 teaspoon freshly ground pepper
¼ cup olive oil
18 large sea scallops, rinsed
   and patted dry (about ½ pound)
1 cup peanut or vegetable oil
Three 6-inch tortillas, preferably blue corn,
   cut into very thin strips
2 cups bitter or peppery greens, such as
   mizuna, arugula, mustard greens, or frisée
½ cup Orange Vinaigrette
1 large ripe mango, peeled, seeded,
   and diced (page 7)

1. Combine the chile powder, cumin, salt, and pepper in a bowl. Set aside.

2. In a sauté pan over high heat, heat the olive oil until it begins to smoke. Slightly dredge the scallops in the chile mixture on one side only. Place the scallops in the heated pan, chile side down, and cook for 20 seconds. Reduce the heat to low, turn the

scallops, and cook for 2 to 3 minutes more. Remove from pan and reserve.

3. In a saucepan over high heat, heat the peanut oil to about 375° F., or until a tortilla strip sizzles when it is immersed. Fry the tortilla strips for 10 to 20 seconds, or until crisp, and drain on paper towels.

4. In a mixing bowl, dress the greens very lightly with the orange vinaigrette. Combine the greens, mango, and tortilla strips, being careful not to break the strips. Divide among 6 individual plates and surround each portion with 3 cooked scallops.

Makes 6 first-course servings

Orange Vinaigrette

1 cup fresh orange juice
2 tablespoons chopped red onion
2 tablespoons fresh lime juice
1 teaspoon Dijon mustard
1 teaspoon ancho chile powder
1 tablespoon red wine vinegar
½ cup olive oil
Salt and freshly ground pepper

1. In a saucepan over high heat, reduce the orange juice until it forms a syrup. Let the syrup cool slightly.

2. In a blender, combine the orange syrup, onion, lime juice, mustard, chile powder, and vinegar. Blend for 30 seconds. With the blender running, slowly add the olive oil until the dressing emulsifies. Season to taste with salt and pepper. Pour into a squeeze bottle. *May be prepared up to 1 day ahead and refrigerated.* Bring to room temperature before serving.

Makes ¾ cup

Grilled Vegetable Salad

with Goat Cheese Croutons & Balsamic Vinaigrette

This salad, electric with color and flavor, is simply a lot of ripe vegetables—red and yellow bell peppers, yellow and green squash, purple eggplant, green broccoli, new potatoes—lightly grilled, dressed with balsamic vinaigrette, and arranged around crisp greens. The goat cheese croutons add extra taste and crunch.

1 medium red bell pepper,
   quartered lengthwise and seeded
1 medium yellow bell pepper,
   quartered lengthwise and seeded
1 medium zucchini, sliced lengthwise
   ¼ inch thick
1 medium yellow squash, sliced
   lengthwise ¼ inch thick
1 baby Italian eggplant, sliced
   lengthwise ¼ inch thick
1 head of broccoli, blanched and
   cut into florets with some
   stem attached (page 7)
4 new potatoes, boiled and sliced
   ¼ inch thick
Olive oil
6 tablespoons Balsamic Vinaigrette
   (recipe opposite)
4 cups mesclun or mixed red and
   green lettuce leaves
8 Goat Cheese Croutons (recipe
   opposite)

1. Prepare a charcoal or wood fire and let it burn down to embers or preheat the broiler. Brush the peppers, zucchini, squash, eggplant, broccoli, and potatoes with olive oil and grill for 2½ minutes on each side, or until grill marks appear. Place in a mixing bowl, dress with ¼ cup of the vinaigrette, and set aside.

2. In a separate mixing bowl, dress the greens with 2 tablespoons of the vinaigrette. Divide the greens equally among 4 plates and arrange the vegetables around the greens, making sure that they are distributed equally. Garnish each portion with 2 goat cheese croutons.

Makes 4 first-course servings

Balsamic Vinaigrette

3 tablespoons balsamic vinegar
1 tablespoon finely chopped red onion
1 tablespoon honey
½ cup olive oil
Salt and freshly ground pepper

In a blender, combine the vinegar, onion, and honey and puree. With the motor running, slowly add the oil until emulsified. Season to taste with salt and pepper and pour into a squeeze bottle. *May be prepared up to 1 day ahead and refrigerated.* Bring to room temperature before serving.
Makes about ¾ cup

Goat Cheese Croutons

Olive oil
8 slices French or Italian bread, ½ inch thick
Salt and freshly ground pepper
8 slices goat cheese, ¼ inch thick
1 tablespoon fresh thyme leaves

1. Preheat the oven to 350° F.
2. Brush both sides of the bread slices with olive oil and sprinkle with salt and pepper. Place the bread on a baking sheet and toast in the oven for about 4 minutes, turning once, until lightly browned.
3. Top each crouton with a slice of goat cheese and sprinkle with thyme, salt, and pepper. Set aside.
Makes 8 croutons

Pan-seared Red Snapper Salad

with Warm Oregano Dressing

This is a one-pan dish. First you sauté the fish and take it out of the pan. Then you heat up the dressing for a split second in the same warm pan and pour the sauce over the fish.

4 red snapper fillets (4 ounces each)
Salt and freshly ground pepper
½ cup olive oil
4 cups mesclun or mixed red and
    green lettuce leaves
¾ cup Oregano Dressing
Cilantro sprigs

1. Season the snapper with salt and pepper to taste. In a medium sauté pan over high heat, heat the olive oil and cook the snapper for about 3 minutes on each side, or until cooked through.

2. Divide the greens among 4 plates. Place 1 piece of cooked snapper over each serving of greens and reserve. Remove the pan from the heat and ladle about ¾ cup of the dressing into the pan. Allow the dressing to warm for 10 seconds, then spoon it over the fish. Garnish with cilantro sprigs.
Makes 4 main-course servings

Oregano Dressing

You need to use fresh—not dried—oregano here.
3 tablespoons capers, drained
½ cup fresh oregano leaves
3 tablespoons fresh lime juice
1 tablespoon minced red onion
1 tablespoon minced garlic
1 teaspoon ancho chile powder
½ cup olive oil
Salt and freshly ground pepper

In a mixing bowl, combine the capers, oregano, lime juice, onion, garlic, and ancho chile powder. Slowly whisk in the oil and season to taste with the salt and pepper. *May be prepared up to 1 day ahead and refrigerated in a squeeze bottle.* Bring to room temperature before serving.
Makes 1 cup

salsas, relishes + sauces

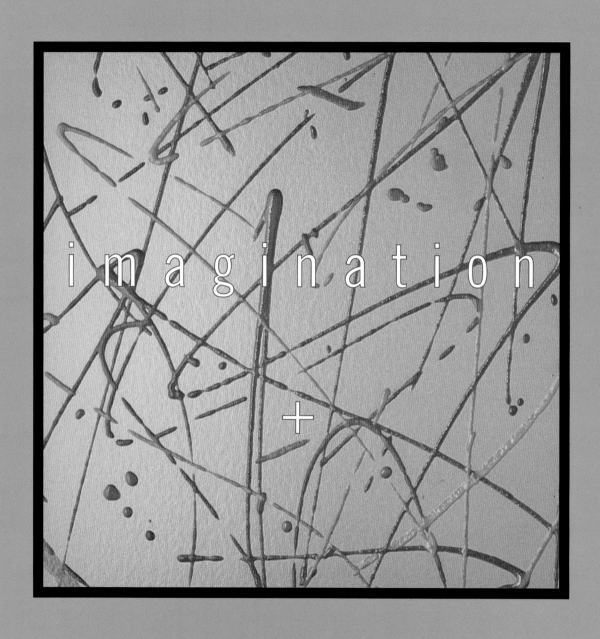

imagination

+

balance

are the  building

blocks

of

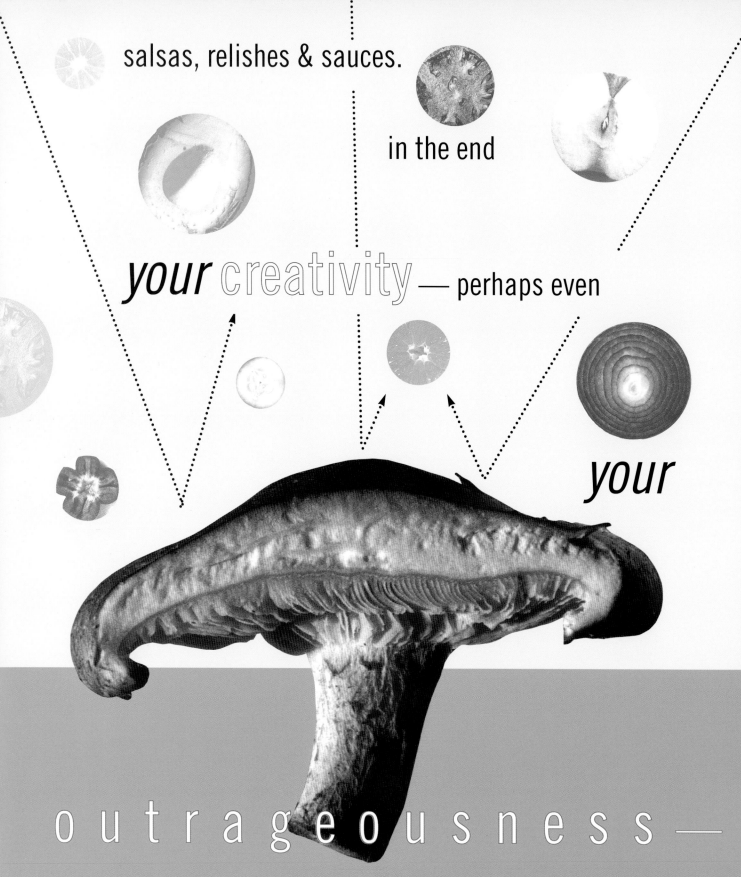

salsas, relishes & sauces.

in the end

your creativity — perhaps even

your

o u t r a g e o u s n e s s —

determines the final result.

W hether you call them salsas (in Spanish) or relishes (in English), these sparkling, chunky mixtures of fruits, herbs, and vegetables are the heart and soul of my cuisine. They are real foods, not just accents. Playing a jazzy counterpoint of piquant and sweet, smooth and crunchy, spicy and cool, they will open your eyes fast, I promise.

In my restaurant kitchen, bowls of freshly prepared salsas are on hand to help in the creation of each dish. They stand lined up on the work counter, ready to transform the simplest foods into show stoppers. In your own kitchen, great dishes are easy to prepare with salsas. Simply cooked fresh fish, poultry, meat, or vegetables become extraordinary when topped with a fresh salsa or relish. And unlike old-fashioned sauces, these salsas are largely low in fat.

On any given day in my kitchen, a cook makes several basic salsas. He or she begins with a basic ingredient, like tomatoes, tomatillos, jalapeño, or papaya, and then adds some onions, cilantro, lime juice, and seasonings. Then it's time to taste, add, mix, and taste again. Like the chunky vinaigrette it is, salsa requires a balance of tartness and mellowness. If it turns out too acidic, a touch of honey or sugar will perfect the mix. After that, anything goes. There is a tremendous range, even within a written recipe, for the cook to collect a bunch of tempting ingredients and improvise. The whole idea is to have a lot of flavors going on in your mouth at the same time. It's all about how *you* want the salsa to taste.

Preparing salsas is simple. Your best kitchen tools are your hands (they mix ingredients without bruising) and your best mind-set is spontaneity.

On page 61, you will find a recipe for Basic Salsa—it's really more guidelines than a recipe—and following that, a recipe for Tomato Salsa. But there are salsas to inspire you all through the book: Tomato and Basil Salsa (page 33); Smoked Tomato Salsa (page 76); Avocado-Tomato Salsa (page 76); four tomatillo-based salsas on pages 78, 122, 134, and 136; Spicy Mango Salsa (page 37); Black Bean–Mango Salsa (page 73); and Black Bean–Corn Salsa (page 84).

Along with salsas and relishes, which are like salsas but thicker, I offer you another piece of kitchen magic, my four "mother sauces": Citrus Vinaigrette, Smoked Yellow Pepper Sauce, Smoked Red Pepper Sauce, and Roasted Poblano Sauce. Use them as foundation sauces on grilled fish, crisp tacos, steaming vegetables—or just about anything—before you spoon on the salsa or glaze.

Imagination and balance are the building blocks of salsas, relishes, and sauces. In the end, your creativity—perhaps even your outrageousness—determines the final result. That's why this food is fun.

salsas, relishes & sauces

that is why this food is fun.

Basic Salsa

With this very simple recipe, you will be able to put together any kind of salsa you can imagine. You can take advantage of the season's ripest tomatoes and peppers, perfect yellow sweet corn that has just come into your local market, or tropical mangoes, papayas, and pineapples.

Every salsa has a main ingredient that provides the controlling flavor. To this you simply add red onion, jalapeño, cilantro, and lime juice. Taste the salsa, and put in some other ingredients if you think they are needed—olive oil for smoothness; more chiles for extra notes of heat and earthy flavor; honey, maple syrup, or sugar to counterbalance any tartness.

All the elements of a salsa should be colorful and fragrant, with perfect, assertive flavor, so that they stand out in combination with each other. Don't throw in anything that isn't ripe—if you cut open a pineapple and it's sour or bland, don't use it. If you can't get fresh chiles or tomatillos, you may substitute good-quality canned ones, and you may use canned black beans. But your main ingredient should be fresh.

As for technique, it's just chop, mix, and taste. Everything in a salsa is cut up, some coarsely chopped, others finely diced or minced. If an ingredient is very spicy or pungent, like garlic or jalapeño, you'll want it cut finer than the main ingredient, be that papaya, mango, pineapple, or tomato. If you feel the salsa needs body, puree half of the main ingredient. This works especially well for mangoes and for tomatillos.

Because freshness is essential to their quality, all uncooked salsas and relishes should be kept, covered and refrigerated, no more than one day.

[Opposite: Clockwise from top, Cranberry Apricot Relish, Tomato and Basil Salsa, Corn and Grilled Pepper Relish, and Tomatillo Salsa

2 cups coarsely chopped main ingredient
2 tablespoons finely diced red onion
2 tablespoons minced jalapeño
¼ cup coarsely chopped cilantro
¼ cup fresh lime juice
Salt and freshly ground white pepper

Combine the main ingredient, onion, jalapeño, cilantro, and lime juice in a bowl, taste, and season to taste with salt and pepper. *Refrigerate, covered, up to 1 day.* Bring to room temperature before serving.

Makes about 3 cups

Tomato Salsa

Even if the tomatoes in your market or garden are less than perfect, they can still make an eye-opening salsa, encouraged by the other ingredients. Just make sure the tomatoes are the freshest you can find. Serve with Blue Corn Chips (page 173) and cold beer.

2 ripe medium tomatoes,
    coarsely chopped
2 tablespoons finely diced red onion
1 tablespoon minced jalapeño
¼ cup fresh lime juice
1 tablespoon ancho chile powder
    or other good-quality chile powder
¼ cup coarsely chopped cilantro
Salt and freshly ground pepper

Combine the tomatoes, onion, jalapeño, lime juice, chile powder, and cilantro in a bowl. Season to taste with salt and pepper. *Refrigerate, covered, for up to 1 day.* Bring to room temperature before serving.

Makes about 2½ cups

White Bean Relish

This is good with grilled fish and Cilantro Pesto (page 77).

    2 cups cooked or canned white beans,
       drained
    2 cup coarsely chopped scallions,
       white and tender green parts
    1 canned chipotle, minced
    ½ cup coarsely chopped fresh
       oregano leaves
    ½ cup fresh lime juice
    ½ cup olive oil
    Salt and freshly ground pepper

Combine the beans, scallions, chipotle, oregano, lime juice, and oil in a bowl, and season with salt and pepper to taste. *Refrigerate for up to 1 day.* Bring to room temperature before serving.
    Makes about 3 cups

Cilantro Oil

When you process the cilantro, it colors the oil a dark chartreuse. Drizzle the oil, or squeeze it out of a plastic squeeze bottle, over Spicy Salmon Tartar (page 93).

    2 cups olive oil
    3 cups (packed) cilantro leaves
    Salt and freshly ground pepper

Combine the olive oil, cilantro, and salt and pepper to taste in a food processor and process for 5 minutes. Strain through a fine strainer. Pour into a bottle or squeeze bottle. *May be prepared up to 3 days ahead, covered, and refrigerated.* Bring to room temperature before serving.
    Makes about 2 cups

Chipotle Mignonette

Mignonette sauce is traditionally served with raw oysters; this version adds the smoky flavor of chipotles to the traditional vinegar and pepper.

    1 cup red wine vinegar
    1 pureed canned chipotle
    1½ tablespoons cracked
       black peppercorns
    2 medium shallots, finely diced
    1 tablespoon coarsely chopped cilantro
    1½ teaspoons honey
    Salt and freshly ground pepper

Combine the vinegar, chipotle, peppercorns, shallots, cilantro, and honey. Season to taste with salt and pepper, and chill. Spoon over freshly opened oysters. This quantity is enough for 24 oysters.
    Makes about 1½ cups

Tomato & Poblano Pepper Relish

Serve this with sautéed halibut or any flaky fish.

- 2 medium tomatoes, coarsely chopped
- 1 poblano, roasted, peeled, seeded, and minced (page 8)
- 3 tablespoons coarsely chopped scallions
- ¼ cup fresh lime juice
- ¼ cup basil chiffonnade
- 3 tablespoons capers, drained
- 3 tablespoons olive oil
- Salt and freshly ground pepper

Combine the tomatoes, poblano, scallions, lime juice, basil, capers, and oil in a bowl and season to taste with salt and pepper. *Refrigerate, covered, for up to 1 day.* Bring to room temperature before serving.

Makes about 3 cups

Smoked Yellow Pepper Oil

In this oil, the ingredients remain separate and visible. The background is saffron-gold, with puddles of deeper gold and highlights of red and green.

- 3 medium yellow bell peppers, cold-smoked (page 7)
- 1 cup olive oil
- 1 teaspoon pureed canned chipotles
- Salt and freshly ground pepper

Process the peppers in a juicer. Pour the juice into a mixing bowl and slowly whisk in the olive oil and chipotle puree. (They do not have to be completely combined; you should be able to see both ingredients.) Season to taste with salt and pepper. Pour into a squeeze bottle. *May be prepared up to 1 day ahead and refrigerated.* Bring to room temperature before serving.

Makes 2 cups

Ginger-Lime Relish

This is terrific with raw oysters.

- 2 cups fresh lime juice
- ¾ cup fresh orange juice
- 2 tablespoons minced ginger
- 1 tablespoon minced garlic
- 1 tablespoon honey
- 3 limes
- ½ cup minced shallots
- 2 tablespoons coarsely chopped cilantro
- Salt and freshly ground pepper

1. In a medium saucepan, combine the juices, ginger, garlic, and honey and bring to a boil over high heat. Reduce by half and set aside to cool.

2. Peel the limes and julienne the zest. Separate the flesh into segments.

3. When the syrup has cooled to room temperature, add the shallots, cilantro, lime segments, and zest. Season to taste with salt and pepper and pour into a nonreactive bowl. *Refrigerate, covered, for up to 1 day.* Bring to room temperature before serving.

Makes about 3 cups

Mother Sauces

In French cuisine, white sauce, brown sauce, and béchamel are called mother sauces, but I rely on a different palette of basics—Citrus Vinaigrette, Smoked Yellow Pepper Sauce, Smoked Red Pepper Sauce, and Roasted Poblano Sauce. I fill plastic squeeze bottles with them and keep them on hand to work magic in my kitchen.

I might drizzle one of these blends over a serving of sizzling fish, hot from the grill, before pairing that fish with its primary sauce. It locks in the natural flavor and juiciness of the fish and adds mysterious notes of its own. Mother sauces impart a hint of flavor to just-cooked vegetables, tacos, or spoonbread, not quite blending with the salsa that follows but enhancing it in a subtle way. These four sauces also can be used without any others, following my suggestions or your own creative ideas.

Roasted Poblano Sauce

May be used on Potato Tacos (page 158), over polenta or spoonbread, and with Grilled Shrimp (page 105). To make the sauce as intense in color as it is in taste, I add a few spinach leaves.

> **2 poblanos, roasted, peeled, and seeded (page 8)**
> **¼ medium red onion, chopped**
> **2 tablespoons fresh lime juice**
> **¾ cup olive oil**
> **½ cup spinach or arugula leaves**
> **2 teaspoons honey**
> **Salt and freshly ground pepper**

In a blender, combine the poblanos, onion, and lime juice and blend until smooth. While the blender is running, add the oil slowly until emulsified. Add the spinach and blend until smooth. Add the honey and season to taste with salt and pepper. *May be prepared up to 1 day ahead and refrigerated in a squeeze bottle.* Bring to room temperature before serving.

Makes about 1½ cups

Smoked Red Pepper Sauce

Be creative with this colorful sauce. Using a squeeze bottle, drizzle it over freshly grilled fish, simple vegetables, or any side dish you choose.

> **2 red bell peppers, cold-smoked, peeled, and seeded (page 7)**
> **¼ medium red onion, coarsely chopped**
> **½ canned chipotle**
> **3 tablespoons fresh lime juice**
> **¾ cup olive oil**
> **Salt and freshly ground pepper**

In a blender, combine the peppers, onion, chipotle, and lime juice and blend until smooth. With the blender running, add the olive oil in a thin stream until the sauce is emulsified. Season to taste. *May be prepared up to 2 days ahead and refrigerated in a squeeze bottle.* Bring to room temperature before serving.

Makes 1 cup

Citrus Vinaigrette

This is the mother sauce of choice for grilled fish, imparting a lemony, sweet flavor and making it juicier. It's especially good with grilled mahimahi.

1 cup fresh orange juice
½ cup fresh lemon juice
½ cup fresh lime juice
2 tablespoons basil chiffonnade
2 tablespoons finely chopped red onion
2 cups olive oil
Salt and freshly ground pepper

In a blender, combine the orange, lemon, and lime juices, basil, and onion and blend. With the motor running, slowly add the olive oil until emulsified. Season to taste with salt and pepper and reserve. *May be prepared up to 2 days ahead and refrigerated in a squeeze bottle.* Bring to room temperature before serving.

Makes 4 cups

Smoked Yellow Pepper Sauce

May be used over fish and vegetables, or try it as a dressing for Southwestern Grilled Tuna Salad (page 47).

2 yellow bell peppers, cold-smoked, peeled, and seeded (page 7)
½ canned chipotle
¼ medium red onion, coarsely chopped
3 tablespoons fresh lime juice
¾ cup olive oil
1 teaspoon sugar
Salt and freshly ground pepper

In a blender, combine the peppers, chipotle, onion, and lime juice and blend. While the blender is running, slowly add the olive oil until emulsified. Add the sugar and salt and pepper to taste. *May be prepared up to 2 days ahead and refrigerated in a squeeze bottle.* Bring to room temperature before serving.

Makes about 1 cup

fish +

i take the   head off to serve the fish

because as hard as it may be to face a whole fish on your plate, it is harder still to

fish and shellfish are my favorite things to cook, probably because they are my favorite things to eat. I keep the cooking simple and I don't doctor my fish—the usual treatment is just olive oil, salt, and pepper before the fish is grilled or sautéed. I never marinate flaky fish like red snapper. Never. Marinating just rips it apart, breaks it down. But sometimes I use a marinade on steak fish or shrimp, which are firm enough to take it.

Steak fish like swordfish, tuna, and mako shark and fillets like mahimahi and halibut are best grilled; the same is true for shrimp and scallops. Preparation is really simple. Light a wood or charcoal fire or preheat the broiler, rub the fish with a little olive oil, and sprinkle it with salt and pepper. Grill until the fish is done to your taste. The degree of doneness depends on the fish: salmon, swordfish, and mahimahi have to be just cooked through, otherwise they will be tough, but tuna should be served rare. Shrimp and scallops need very little time on the fire.

Another good way to prepare fillets is pan-frying, using a skillet that holds them with a little space around each, so that they don't touch. Never dredge the fish in flour. Just turn your stove up high, heat some olive oil in a skillet, and add a bit of butter to color the fish. When the fish has colored and is crusty on one side, turn down the heat, turn over the fish, and finish cooking it on the other side. Gas heat works better than electric heat for pan-frying fish, because the heating elements on an electric range remain hot even after you turn them down. But on an electric range, you can brown the fillets on one side, turn them, and then finish cooking them in a preheated 350° F. oven. Although you get a different kind of cooking in the oven because the heat is not direct, finishing them this way allows the fillets to cook through without burning. Another option is to take the pan off the heat while the element cools and then return it to the stove; or you could move the pan to an element that is set at a lower temperature. The idea is to brown the fillets on one side and then let them cook slowly through without burning.

For an exotic dish, red snapper fillets can be wrapped in banana leaves and roasted. Cooked this way, the fish is partly roasted and partly steamed, and very flavorful.

I like to roast whole fish, like baby red snapper or baby black sea bass. Unboned fish is unbelievable, flaky and moist and sweet. I take the head off before serving fish because most people find it hard to look a fish in the eye.

Lobster is tastiest when it is roasted, too. Simply place the split lobsters on a baking pan, shell side down, brush with olive oil, and roast them for 15 to 20 minutes.

Shrimp and scallops taste best and retain their juiciness when quickly grilled. Squid takes very well to frying in lightly seasoned cornmeal batter. For oysters, I like a spicy cornmeal coating, then a fast bath in hot oil.

You can also "cook" fish or shellfish without any heat if you cover it with lime juice and let it marinate for three to four hours. The lime juice prevents spoilage. My recipe for ceviche combines scallops, salmon, shrimp, red onions, mangoes, tomatoes, and

look it in the  eye.

citrus fruit segments. You can also forget about cooking altogether when you serve salmon tartar with a flavored oil.

The actual grilling, sautéing, or roasting is the simplest part of each recipe in this chapter. The fish and seafood are cooked quickly and allowed to retain their natural character. Then they are adorned and electrified by sauces, salsas, and relishes. I pair Grilled Tuna with Black Bean–Mango Salsa and Avocado Vinaigrette and I serve Grilled Swordfish with a Red Onion Marmalade, for example. I take roasted lobster meat, add Corn Relish, fold it into a blue corn pancake, and spoon on some hot Red Curry Sauce.

To give your own signature to each dish, drizzle fish with a mother sauce—Smoked Yellow or Red Pepper or Roasted Poblano Sauce or Citrus Vinaigrette (pages 64–65) — before you add a salsa or relish. Keep these sauces in plastic bottles and squeeze them over the top of the fish, after you have put it on the plate.

This is a great way to cook. It is easy and it lends itself to preparing in stages. It is seasonal—you can use perfect tomatoes and corn, for instance, when they are at their peak—but also independent of the seasons since many salsa and relish ingredients are plentiful all year round. It allows you to break loose with spices and herbs to your taste. The fish is sizzling, the sauces are bold—what could be better?

The key to spectacular fish dishes is getting great fish. If your purchase isn't perfect, throw it out and start over. How can you judge freshness and quality in fish? It depends on each type: tuna steaks should be bright red; swordfish should be shiny and firm; and snapper should be firm, not mushy, with very little fish odor. The light, briny smell, firmness, and clear, shiny flesh of fresh fish are unmistakable. If you can say to yourself, "What a beautiful fish!" buy it.

fish & shellfish

if you can say to yourself, "what a beautiful then buy it

Cornmeal-coated Squid

Cornmeal-coated squid is Southwestern calamari. Serve it with Green Chile Aioli (page 96) or Spicy and Sweet Dipping Sauce.

- 1½ cups dark beer (12-ounce can)
- 2 large eggs, lightly beaten
- ½ cup milk
- 2½ cups all-purpose flour
- 6 squid, cleaned and sliced into rings
- 8 tablespoons (1 stick) unsalted butter, melted
- 1 cup seasoned cornmeal (page 6)
- 4 cups peanut oil

1. In a mixing bowl, combine the beer, eggs, milk, and 1½ cups of the flour. Pour the remaining 1 cup of flour into 1 bowl and the cornmeal into another. Dredge the squid in the plain flour, dip in the beer batter, and dredge in the seasoned cornmeal.

2. In a large saucepan over high heat, heat the oil to 375° F., or until a piece of squid sizzles when immersed. Fry the squid for 4 minutes, or until crisp. Drain on paper towels and serve immediately.

Makes 6 servings

Spicy & Sweet Dipping Sauce

- 1½ cups red wine vinegar
- ½ cup sugar
- 1 teaspoon chopped jalapeño
- 1 tablespoon plus 1 teaspoon finely chopped ginger
- ¼ cup rice wine vinegar
- ¼ cup fresh lime juice
- 1 tablespoon sesame oil
- 1 tablespoon finely chopped mint
- 1 tablespoon finely chopped basil
- 1 tablespoon finely chopped cilantro
- 2 tablespoons finely diced red bell pepper
- 2 tablespoons finely diced yellow bell pepper
- 2 tablespoons finely diced poblano

1. In a medium saucepan over high heat, combine the red wine vinegar, sugar, jalapeño, and 1 teaspoon of the ginger and bring to a boil. Reduce to a thick syrup and strain into a mixing bowl. Let cool to room temperature.

2. Add the rice wine vinegar, lime juice, and sesame oil and mix well. Add the remaining 1 tablespoon of ginger and the remaining ingredients. *May be prepared up to 2 days ahead, covered, and refrigerated.* Bring to room temperature before serving.

Makes 2½ cups

Grilled Tuna Steaks

Tuna steaks should be cut one-and-a-half to two inches thick and cooked rare. Once this fish is over-cooked even a bit, it becomes tough and dry. Top quality is imperative for tuna, even more so than for other fish, precisely because you're cooking it rare. It is delicious served with Spicy Mango Glaze.

2 tablespoons olive oil
Salt and freshly ground black pepper
4 tuna steaks (6 ounces each)

1. Prepare a wood or charcoal fire and let it burn down to embers or preheat the broiler.

2. Rub the steaks with olive oil and season to taste with salt and pepper. Grill or broil for 2 minutes on each side for rare, or to taste. Serve immediately.

Makes 4 servings

Spicy Mango Glaze

1½ cups red wine vinegar
½ cup sugar
1 teaspoon finely chopped jalapeño
1 teaspoon finely peeled ginger
**1 ripe mango, peeled, seeded, and
   roughly sliced (page 7)**
Salt and freshly ground pepper

1. In a medium saucepan over medium heat, combine the vinegar, sugar, jalapeño, and ginger. Cook, stirring occasionally, until thick and caramelized. When the sauce just turns golden brown, immediately remove the pan from the heat and strain into a bowl. Let it cool at room temperature.

2. In a blender, puree the mango. Pour it into a bowl and add the cooled caramel. Season to taste with salt and freshly ground pepper. *May be prepared up to 2 days ahead, covered, and refrigerated.* Bring to room temperature before serving.

Makes about 1 cup

Grilled Tuna Tostada

with Black Bean– Mango Salsa & Avocado Vinaigrette

Tostadas usually are vehicles for beans and cheeses and salady things. This is a more contemporary dish, pairing them with grilled tuna. You can serve this dish as a dinner appetizer or a lunch entree.

2 cups peanut oil
Six 4-inch flour tortillas, cut from
 6-inch tortillas
¾ cup Black Bean–Mango Salsa, at room
 temperature
Grilled Tuna Steaks (preceding recipe)
6 tablespoons Avocado Vinaigrette, at
 room temperature

1. In a medium skillet over high heat, heat the peanut oil to 375° F. or until an edge of a tortilla sizzles when it is immersed. Fry the tortillas until crisp, about 1½ minutes on each side. Drain on paper towels and set aside.

2. For each tostada, spread 1 tortilla with a thin layer of salsa and top with a piece of grilled tuna. Drizzle avocado vinaigrette over the top and serve.
 Makes 6 servings

Black Bean–Mango Salsa

You can transform this into a Black Bean–Papaya Salsa by substituting an equal amount of papaya for the mango.

1 cup cooked or canned black beans,
 drained
1 medium mango, peeled and coarsely
 chopped (about 1 cup)
½ cup finely chopped red onion
1 jalapeño, stemmed, seeded, and
 finely diced
½ cup coarsely chopped cilantro
½ cup fresh lime juice
¼ cup olive oil
Salt and freshly ground white pepper

 Combine the beans, mango, onion, jalapeño, cilantro, lime juice, and oil in a bowl. Season to taste with salt and pepper. *May be prepared and refrigerated, covered, up to 1 day ahead.* Bring to room temperature 1 hour before serving.
Makes about 2½ cups

Avocado Vinaigrette

½ Haas avocado, peeled
½ jalapeño, seeded
2 tablespoons finely chopped red onion
¼ cup fresh lime juice
1 teaspoon sugar
1 cup olive oil
Salt and freshly ground white pepper

 1. In a blender, puree the avocado, jalapeño, onion, lime juice, and sugar until smooth.

 2. With the motor running, slowly add the oil until it emulsifies. *May be prepared up to 1 day ahead and refrigerated, covered, in a nonreactive bowl.* Bring to room temperature 1 hour before serving. Serve extra avocado vinaigrette in a bowl in the center of the table.
Makes 1½ cups

Red Pepper–crusted Tuna Steak

with Spicy Mango Salsa

Freshly ground chiles and peppercorns form a spicy crust for tuna, much as they do for filet mignon (page 118). The mango salsa adds a cool accent to the fiery fish.

2 New Mexico reds
1 tablespoon black peppercorns
6 tuna steaks (6 ounces each)
½ cup olive oil
Salt
6 tablespoons Spicy Mango Salsa, or
   to taste (page 37)

1. In a coffee grinder or spice grinder, coarsely grind the chiles and peppercorns together. Dredge the tuna steaks in the pepper mixture on one side only.

2. In a large sauté pan over medium-high heat, heat the olive oil until it begins to smoke and cook the tuna, pepper side down, for 1 minute, or until a crust forms. Lower the heat to medium, turn the steaks, and cook for 3 minutes more. The fish should be rare. Season to taste with salt.

3. For each serving, place 1 steak on a plate, pepper side up, with salsa to taste. Serve immediately.
   Makes 6 servings

G r i l l e d   S w o r d f i s h

Buy swordfish steaks cut about 1 inch thick or thicker but never thinner. Grill until the fish is just cooked through and no longer, otherwise it will be tough. Serve with Cilantro Pesto, Avocado-Tomato Salsa, or Red Onion Marmalade (recipes follow).

4 swordfish steaks (6 ounces each)
2 tablespoons olive oil
Salt and freshly ground black pepper

1. Prepare a wood or charcoal fire and let it burn down to embers, or preheat the broiler.

2. Rub the steaks with olive oil and season with salt and pepper. Grill or broil for 4 minutes on each side, or until lightly browned. Serve immediately, with accompaniments to taste.

Makes 4 servings

Avocado-Tomato Salsa

Another good topping for swordfish is this salsa, full of the flavors of summer.

1 Haas avocado, coarsely chopped
1 medium tomato, coarsely chopped
1 tablespoon finely diced red onion
1 to 2 teaspoons finely diced jalapeño
2 tablespoons fresh lime juice
Salt and freshly ground white pepper

Taking care not to break up the avocado too much, combine it with the tomato, onion, jalapeño, and lime juice in a bowl. Season to taste with salt and pepper. Cover and reserve. *May be prepared up to 6 hours ahead, covered, and refrigerated.* Bring to room temperature before serving.

Makes about 1½ cups

Cilantro Pesto

Top each swordfish steak with about two table-spoons of this refreshing pesto. This is good fare for people who want Southwestern taste but don't want a spicy dish.

2 cups (firmly packed) cilantro leaves
2 garlic cloves
2 tablespoons pumpkin seeds
2 tablespoons fresh lime juice
2 teaspoons salt
1 teaspoon freshly ground black pepper
5 tablespoons olive oil

In a food processor, combine the cilantro, garlic, pumpkin seeds, lime juice, salt, and pepper. With the motor running, slowly add the olive oil until the sauce is emulsified. *May be prepared up to 2 days ahead, covered, and refrigerated.* Bring to room temperature 1 hour before serving.

Makes 1 cup

Red Onion Marmalade

This unusual sweet-and-sour marmalade goes well with any grilled steak fish.

3 tablespoons unsalted butter
5 medium red onions, sliced
**   thin crosswise**
1½ cups red wine vinegar
½ cup crème de cassis
½ cup grenadine
½ cup red wine
½ cup coarsely chopped cilantro
Salt and freshly ground white pepper

In a large saucepan over medium heat, melt the butter and sweat the onions for 3 minutes. Add the vinegar, cassis, grenadine, and wine and reduce until the liquid has almost entirely evaporated and the onions are glazed. Add the cilantro and season to taste with salt and pepper. *May be prepared up to 1 day ahead of time, covered, and refrigerated.* Bring to room temperature 1 hour before serving. Serve extra in a bowl in the center of the table.

Makes about 3 cups

fish & shellfish

Grilled Mahimahi

Mahimahi, a fish from tropical waters. is available in fillets that are firm and flavorful. It should be cooked just through for the best texture. The flavor of pineapple goes very well with mahimahi. Try the fish topped with Pineapple-Tomatillo Salsa or Pineapple-Red Onion Relish. A little citrus vinaigrette drizzled on top (about ½ cup for 6 fillets) will enhance its sweetness.

4 mahimahi fillets (6 ounces each)
2 tablespoons olive oil
Salt and freshly ground black pepper

1. Prepare a wood or charcoal fire and let it burn down to embers, or preheat the broiler.

2. Rub the fillets with olive oil and season to taste with salt and pepper. Grill or broil for 4 minutes on each side, or until lightly browned. Serve immediately.

Makes 4 servings

Pineapple-Tomatillo Salsa

Top the mahimahi with about 2 tablespoons of this salsa. Be sure your pineapple is ripe and fragrant.

½ cup coarsely chopped fresh ripe pineapple
½ cup finely diced tomatillo
1½ tablespoons coarsely chopped cilantro
3 tablespoons fresh lime juice
¼ medium red onion, chopped fine
¼ jalapeño, seeded and chopped fine
2 tablespoons olive oil
Salt and freshly ground pepper

Combine the pineapple, tomatillo, cilantro, lime juice, onion, jalapeño, and olive oil. Season to taste with salt and pepper. Cover and reserve. *May be prepared up to 1 day in advance, covered, and refrigerated.* Bring to room temperature 1 hour before serving. Serve extra salsa in a bowl in the center of the table.

Makes 1½ cups

Pineapple–Red Onion Relish

Serve this relish with mahimahi or with Red Chile Duck (page 128).

½ cup medium-diced fresh pineapple
¼ cup thinly sliced red onion
½ jalapeño, minced
1½ teaspoons coarsely chopped cilantro
1 tablespoon fresh lime juice
1 tablespoon rice wine vinegar
Salt and freshly ground pepper

Place the pineapple, onion, jalapeño, cilantro, lime juice, and vinegar in a mixing bowl and mix well with a plastic spatula. Season to taste with salt and pepper. *May be prepared up to 1 day ahead of time, covered, and refrigerated.* Bring to room temperature 1 hour before serving.

Makes about 1½ cups

Grilled Halibut

Halibut is among my favorite fish, with a great texture—flaky, but with a good meaty consistency—and a neutral flavor that can go with bold flavors. Halibut cooks faster than you think, so take it off the heat 30 seconds before you think it is done. Serve it with a delicate Curried Corn Sauce or with a Tomato and Roasted Poblano Sauce (recipe opposite) with more kick.

6 halibut fillets (6 ounces each)
3 tablespoons olive oil
Salt and freshly ground black pepper

1. Prepare a wood or charcoal fire and let it burn down to embers, or preheat the broiler.

2. Rub the fillets with olive oil and season to taste with salt and pepper. Grill or broil for about 3 minutes on each side. Serve immediately.

Makes 6 servings

Curried Corn Sauce

2 tablespoons butter
¼ cup coarsely chopped onion
½ medium green apple, sliced
1½ teaspoons chopped garlic
¼ cup Curry Powder (page 6)
2 cups Fish Stock (page 16)
1 cup fresh corn kernels
½ cup heavy cream
Salt and freshly ground
**   pepper to taste**

1. In a medium saucepan over medium heat, melt 1 tablespoon of the butter and add the onion, apple, garlic, and curry powder. Sauté until the onion is translucent. Add the stock, bring to a boil, and simmer, covered, for 1 hour. Strain the stock through a fine strainer into a bowl and discard the solids.

2. In a medium saucepan over medium heat, melt the remaining butter and cook the corn until heated through. Add the curried stock and simmer, covered, for 45 minutes.

3. In a small saucepan over medium-high heat, bring the cream to a boil. Simmer until reduced by three-fourths. Add the reduced cream to the stock and simmer, covered, for 10 minutes. Remove from the heat and season to taste with salt and pepper. *May be made up to 2 days ahead and refrigerated, covered.* Reheat, stirring, just before serving.

Makes 4 cups

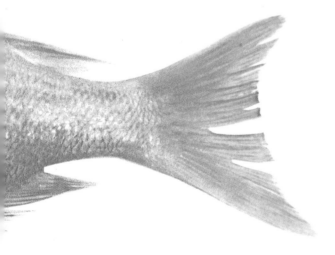

Tomato & Roasted Poblano Sauce

Fresh tomatoes give this sauce a spirited flavor and canned tomatoes give it a strong base.

2 tablespoons olive oil
¼ medium red onion, cut into small dice
1 tablespoon minced garlic
½ cup red wine
3 canned plum tomatoes, roughly chopped
2 medium fresh tomatoes, peeled, seeded, and cut into 1-inch dice
1 roasted poblano, peeled, seeded, and cut into 2-inch dice (page 8)
1½ tablespoons basil chiffonnade
½ teaspoon sugar
Salt and freshly ground pepper

1. In a medium saucepan over medium heat, heat the olive oil and sweat the onion and garlic for 3 minutes. Raise the heat to high, add the wine, bring to a boil, and reduce to 1 tablespoon. Add the tomatoes and poblano and bring back to a boil.

2. Reduce the heat to medium and simmer for 20 minutes, or until smooth. Add the basil and sugar and season to taste with salt and pepper. *May be prepared up to 2 days ahead and refrigerated in a squeeze bottle.* Bring to room temperature before serving.

Makes 1 cup

Pan-fried Halibut Fillets

with Roasted Vegetable– Green Chile Broth

Don't use any flour on the fillets before you pan-fry them—just season lightly with a little salt and pepper. Cook them quickly and serve immediately. This broth is light, yet hearty with its colorful roasted vegetables. Each fillet swims in a generous puddle.

> 4 cups Roasted Vegetable–Green Chile
> Broth
> 2 tablespoons olive oil
> ½ teaspoon unsalted butter
> 6 halibut fillets (about 6 ounces each)
> Salt and freshly ground pepper

1. Prepare or reheat the broth.

2. In a medium skillet over medium-high heat, heat the oil until it begins to smoke and then add the butter. Season the fillets with salt and pepper to taste on both sides and cook for 2 to 3 minutes on each side. (If you have an electric range, brown the fillets on 1 side, turn them, and finish cooking in a preheated 350° F. oven for 3 minutes.)

3. Place 1 halibut fillet in each of 6 soup bowls and pour broth around it.

Makes 6 servings

Roasted Vegetable– Green Chile Broth

See page 8 for directions for roasting vegetables.

> **1 tablespoon unsalted butter**
> **1 tablespoon finely diced red onion**
> **1 tablespoon finely diced roasted garlic**
> **½ cup white wine**
> **2 cups Fish Stock (page 16)**
> **½ roasted red bell pepper,**
> **seeded and peeled**
> **½ roasted yellow bell pepper,**
> **seeded and peeled**
> **1 roasted poblano, seeded and peeled**
> **8 cloves roasted garlic**
> **12 roasted shallots**
> **12 roasted pearl onions**
> **Salt and freshly ground pepper**
> **Honey**

In a medium saucepan over medium heat, melt the butter and sweat the onion and garlic. Add the wine, raise the heat to high, and reduce the liquid completely. Reduce the heat to medium, add the stock, roasted peppers, poblano, garlic, shallots, and pearl onions, and simmer for 30 minutes. Puree the mixture in a blender or processor, or in the pan with a hand-held blender. Season to taste with salt, pepper, and honey. *May be made up to 2 days ahead and refrigerated, covered.* Reheat, stirring, just before serving.

Makes 4 cups

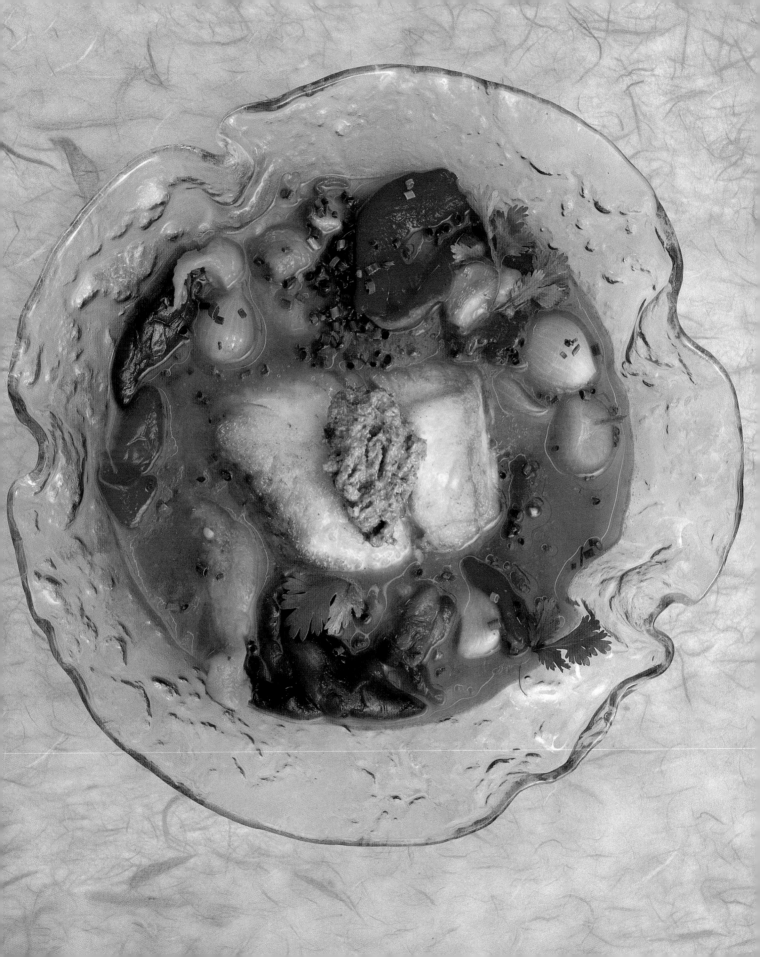

Grilled Salmon

Salmon fillets should be cooked to about medium, when they will be firm on the outside and soft on the inside, even a touch raw in the middle. Salmon stands up well to spicy sauces and glazes, like Black Bean–Corn Salsa or Ancho Chile–Honey Glaze. It's also good with Tomatillo-Chipotle Sauce (recipe opposite) or Tomato–New Mexico Red Chile Sauce (page 95).

4 salmon fillets (6 ounces each)
2 tablespoons olive oil
Salt and freshly ground black pepper

1. Prepare a wood or charcoal fire and let it burn down to embers, or preheat the broiler.

2. Rub the fillets with olive oil and season to taste with salt and pepper. Grill or broil for 4 minutes on each side, or until lightly browned. Serve immediately.

Makes 4 servings

Ancho Chile–Honey Glaze

Spoon a little of this sweet-and-spicy glaze over grilled salmon for a touch of heat.

½ cup honey
2 tablespoons Dijon mustard
2 tablespoons ancho chile powder
Salt and freshly ground pepper

Combine the honey, mustard, and chile powder in a bowl. Season to taste with salt and pepper. *May be prepared up to 2 weeks in advance, covered, and refrigerated.* Bring to room temperature before serving. Thin with a little water if necessary.

Makes ¾ cup

Black Bean–Corn Salsa

The great colors of this salsa atop the pink salmon are almost reason enough to put together this dish; it can be a complete summer meal, besides. It is one of my first Southwestern combinations.

½ cup cooked or canned black beans, drained
½ cup roasted corn kernels (page 8)
2 tablespoons finely diced red onion
½ tablespoon finely diced jalapeño
2 tablespoons fresh lime juice
2 tablespoons basil chiffonnade
2 tablespoons olive oil
Salt and freshly ground pepper

Combine the beans, corn, onion, jalapeño, lime juice, basil, and olive oil in a bowl. Stir and season to taste with salt and pepper. Cover and set aside. *May be prepared up to 1 day in advance, covered, and refrigerated.* Bring to room temperature before serving.

Makes about 1¼ cups

Tomatillo-Chipotle Sauce

A spoonful of this tart and fiery sauce with its smoky aftertaste gives grilled salmon a new twist.

6 medium tomatillos, husked
2 garlic cloves, peeled
½ medium red onion, peeled
  and quartered
1½ tablespoons olive oil
1 canned chipotle
¼ cup cilantro leaves
1½ teaspoons honey
Salt and freshly ground pepper

1. Preheat the oven to 350° F.

2. Rub the tomatillos, garlic, and onion with the olive oil, place on a baking sheet, and roast for 20 minutes, or until the tomatillos are soft but still green.

3. In a blender or processor, puree the roasted vegetables with the chipotles, cilantro, honey, and salt and pepper to taste. *May be prepared up to 1 day in advance, covered, and refrigerated.* Bring to room temperature before serving.

Makes 1 cup

Tequila-cured Salmon Tostada

with Black Bean–Mango Salsa & Avocado Vinaigrette

I love this dish. All the flavors work perfectly together. The salsa and vinaigrette combination is also wonderful with tuna (page 73).

2 cups peanut oil
Six 4-inch flour tortillas, cut from 6-inch
  tortillas
¾ cup Black Bean–Mango Salsa
  (page 73)
12 paper-thin slices Tequila-cured
  Salmon (page 87)
¾ cup Avocado Vinaigrette (page 73)

1. In a large saucepan over high heat, heat the oil to 375° F, or until a piece of tortilla sizzles when it is immersed. Fry the tortillas until crisp, about 1½ minutes on each side. Drain on paper towels and set aside.

2. For each tostada, place 1 fried tortilla on a plate and cover with a thin layer of salsa, 2 slices of salmon, and 2 tablespoons of vinaigrette. Serve immediately.

Makes 6 first-course servings

Blue Corn Pancakes

with Smoked Salmon & Mango-Serrano Crème Fraîche

Smoked salmon, pancakes, and crème fraîche—classic, yes, but here sweet and spicy flavors liven things up. Serve this as an appetizer or for lunch.

BLUE CORN PANCAKES:
½ cup blue cornmeal
½ cup all-purpose flour
¼ tablespoon baking powder
2 tablespoons honey
Salt
1 large egg, lightly beaten
½ cup plus 2 tablespoons milk
1 tablespoon unsalted butter, melted

Vegetable oil
4 slices smoked salmon
1¾ cups Mango-Serrano crème fraîche
Cilantro leaves

1. In a mixing bowl, combine the cornmeal, flour, baking powder, honey, and a pinch of salt. In a separate bowl, combine the egg, milk, and melted butter. Add the egg mixture to the dry ingredients and mix well. *May be prepared up to 2 days ahead and refrigerated.*

2. Heat a griddle or cast-iron frying pan over high heat, brush with oil, and add ¼ cup batter for each pancake. Fry for about 1 minute, or until dry around the edges, turn, and fry for about 30 seconds until cooked through. *May be prepared up to 4 hours ahead.*

3. To serve, place a pancake on each plate, spoon 1 tablespoon crème fraîche over it, and place 1 slice of smoked salmon on top. Roll the pancake as you would a crêpe and garnish with a few cilantro leaves and the remaining crème fraîche.

Makes 4 servings

Mango-Serrano Crème Fraîche

Crème fraîche would dilute the flavor of a lesser chile, so I went all out and added some highly spicy serranos to this sauce.

1¼ cups crème fraîche (page 6)
   or regular or light sour cream
1 ripe mango, peeled, seeded,
   and finely diced (page 7)
2 roasted serranos, finely diced (page 8)
½ medium red onion, finely diced
Salt and freshly ground black pepper

Combine the crème fraîche, mango, serranos, and onion. Season to taste with salt and pepper. Cover and refrigerate up to 1 day.

Makes 1¾ cups

Tequila-cured Salmon

Here is my Southwestern version of gravlax, full of the intricate flavors of tequila, cilantro, mustard seeds, and chipotles.

> 1 salmon fillet, skin on (about 2 pounds)
> 1 tablespoon canned pureed chipotles
> ¼ cup chopped cilantro
> ¼ cup whole mustard seeds
> 2 tablespoons cumin seeds
> Zest of 5 limes, in strips
> 2 cups kosher salt
> 3 cups (packed) light brown sugar
> 1 cup tequila

1. Place the salmon fillet on a baking sheet, flesh side up. Spread with pureed chipotles. Sprinkle evenly with cilantro, mustard seeds, cumin seeds, and lime zest.

2. In a mixing bowl, combine the salt, brown sugar, and tequila. Cover the salmon with the salt mixture.

3. Place another baking sheet on top of the salmon and weight it down with a cutting board or similar weight. Refrigerate for 48 hours.

4. Remove from the refrigerator and scrape off the curing ingredients. When cured, the fish should have a raw appearance and a firm but not hard texture. If the color changes to pale pink, the curing has gone on for too long, and the fish is "cooked."

5. Slice the salmon against the grain paper thin and serve.

Makes about 40 slices

Tequila-cured Salmon with Whole-grain Mustard Cream

Traditionally gravlax is served with dark bread or flatbread and mustard. Our flatbread is flavored with blue corn, and this mustard is a creamy, whole-grain sauce with chopped cilantro. The plate is then garnished with sprigs of cilantro.

> 24 paper-thin slices Tequila-cured Salmon
> 6 tablespoons Whole-grain Mustard Cream
> 1 recipe Blue Corn Flatbread (page 168)
> 12 cilantro sprigs

On each of 6 plates arrange 4 slices of salmon along the top and a pile of flatbread pieces along the bottom, separated by a puddle of mustard cream.

Makes 6 first-course servings

Whole-grain Mustard Cream

> 3½ tablespoons whole-grain mustard
> 1½ tablespoons sour cream or crème fraîche (page 6)
> 1 tablespoon chopped cilantro
> Salt and freshly ground pepper

Combine the mustard, sour cream, and cilantro. Season to taste with salt and pepper. Cover and refrigerate. Bring to room temperature before serving.

Makes 6 tablespoons

New Mexico–Style Barbecued Salmon

Salmon pairs well with a dark barbecue sauce that is full of deep chile flavor.

    4 salmon fillets (6 ounces each)
    New Mexico–style Barbecue Sauce
      (page 36)

1. Two hours before cooking, brush the salmon fillets on both sides with the sauce and refrigerate.

2. Prepare a charcoal or wood fire and allow it to burn down to embers, or preheat the broiler. Grill or broil the salmon for 2 to 3 minutes on each side, or until lightly browned. Brush again with barbecue sauce, and serve immediately.

Makes 4 servings

New Mexico–Style Barbecued Salmon with Southwest Potato Salad, opposite

Blue Corn Salmon Cakes with Pineapple-Tomatillo Salsa

These salmon cakes are similar to crab cakes, but with the crunchiness and corn flavor of blue cornmeal and the bold note of horseradish. Pineapple-Tomatillo Salsa adds the perfect accent. Serve these cakes as an appetizer.

    2 pounds fresh salmon fillets
    6 tablespoons olive oil
    1 medium red onion, diced
    2 jalapeños, diced
    3 tablespoons prepared horseradish, drained
    ¼ cup Dijon mustard
    3 tablespoons crème fraîche (page 62),
      sour cream or plain yogurt
    1 large egg, lightly beaten
    Salt and freshly ground pepper
    1 cup blue cornmeal
    1 cup Pineapple-Tomatillo Salsa (page 78)

1. In a medium pan over medium heat, poach the salmon for 8 minutes in lightly salted simmering water to cover. Remove, cool slightly, and flake the fish. Set aside.

2. In a skillet over low to medium heat, heat 2 tablespoons olive oil and sauté the onion and jalapeños until translucent. Remove from the heat and set aside.

3. In a mixing bowl, combine the salmon, onion mixture, horseradish, mustard, crème fraîche, egg, and salt and pepper to taste. Refrigerate, covered, for 1 hour or up to 1 day.

4. Form the chilled salmon mixture into 2-inch patties ½ inch thick and dredge in cornmeal. Heat the remaining 4 tablespoons olive oil in a large skillet over medium heat and fry the cakes for about 3 minutes on each side, or until crusty and lightly browned.

5. Serve immediately with the salsa spooned on top.

Makes 12 cakes

Red Chile–crusted Salmon Steaks

with Smoked Yellow Pepper Sauce

You can dredge a thick salmon steak in ground chiles and then sear it. Serve it with a cool pepper sauce for contrast.

¼ cup ancho chile powder
2 tablespoons ground cumin
Salt and freshly ground black pepper
6 salmon steaks (about 6 ounces each)
½ cup olive oil
¾ cup Smoked Yellow Pepper Sauce
  (page 65)

1. In a mixing bowl, combine the ancho chile powder, cumin, and salt and pepper to taste. Dredge the salmon steaks in the mixture on one side only.

2. In a large sauté pan over high heat, heat the olive oil until it begins to smoke. Cook the salmon steaks, pepper side down, for about 1 minute, or until a crust forms. Lower the heat to medium, turn the steaks, and cook for 5 minutes more. The fish should be rare to medium.

3. For each serving, place 1 steak on a plate, pepper side up, and drizzle with the pepper sauce.
Makes 6 servings

Spicy Salmon Tartar
with Cilantro Oil & Plantain Croutons

Serve salmon tartar as an appetizer or with drinks, and eat it on crisp Plantain Croutons dipped into the spicy mixture.

> ¾ pound salmon, cut into ¼-inch dice (2 cups)
> 2 tablespoons Dijon mustard
> 2 tablespoons pureed canned chipotles
> ¼ cup capers, drained
> ¼ cup finely chopped scallions
> 2 tablespoons olive oil
> 2 tablespoons Cilantro Oil (page 62)
> 1 recipe Plantain Croutons (page 173)

In a mixing bowl, combine all the ingredients except the cilantro oil and croutons. Mix well. Serve immediately, drizzled with cilantro oil and garnished with plantain croutons.

Makes 6 servings

Pan-Fried Red Snapper

American red snapper is sometimes hard to find, but it is the best, so ask for it at your fish market. Some of the imported snapper is hardly worth bothering about, and you may want to substitute halibut or sea bass if only the imports are available. Cook the fish naturally—never dredge it in flour before frying. The snapper is particularly good with my Charred Jalapeño–Basil Vinaigrette or Tomato–New Mexico Red Chile Sauce (recipe opposite).

> **2 tablespoons olive oil**
> **½ teaspoon unsalted butter**
> **Salt and freshly ground pepper**
> **6 red snapper fillets (about 6 ounces each)**

In a medium skillet over medium heat, heat the oil until it begins to smoke and then add the butter. Season the fillets on both sides with salt and pepper to taste. Cook for 2 to 3 minutes per side, starting with the skin side down. (If you have an electric range, brown the fillets on 1 side, turn them, and finish cooking in a preheated 350° F. oven for 3 minutes.) Remove the cooked fillets to a warm plate and serve immediately.

Makes 6 servings

Charred Jalapeño–Basil Vinaigrette

As soon as the snapper comes off the pan, hit it with the vinaigrette (which has to be at room temperature). The vinaigrette heats up on the fish and all the flavors spring to life.

1 tablespoon olive oil
1 jalapeño pepper
2 tablespoons diced red onion
1 tablespoon minced garlic
1 tablespoon Dijon mustard
1 tablespoon red wine vinegar
1 tablespoon balsamic vinegar
1 tablespoon rice wine vinegar
1 cup olive oil
1 tablespoon sesame oil
2 tablespoons basil chiffonnade
1 tablespoon ancho chile powder
Salt and freshly ground black pepper

1. In a small sauté pan over high heat, heat the olive oil and cook the jalapeño on all sides until the skin is charred. Let the pepper cool and then slice it thin, including the seeds and stem.

2. In a large mixing bowl, combine the remaining ingredients, including salt and pepper to taste, with the jalapeño and whisk until blended. *May be prepared 6 hours ahead, covered, and refrigerated.* Bring to room temperature before serving.

3. Spoon the charred jalapeño–basil vinaigrette to taste over the fish as soon as you take it from the pan and serve immediately.

Makes 2 cups

Tomato–New Mexico Red Chile Sauce

Infuse tomato sauce with a red chile puree to give it a little more spice and a deeper flavor. This sauce is also good with grilled salmon or as a dip for blue corn tortilla strips.

1 tablespoon unsalted butter
2 tablespoons finely chopped red onion
4 cloves roasted garlic, chopped (page 8)
One 8-ounce can tomatoes, seeded and drained
4 ancho chiles, rehydrated and pureed (page 8)
Salt and freshly ground pepper
3 tablespoons crème fraîche (page 6)

1. In a small saucepan over medium heat, melt the butter and sweat the onion and garlic. Add the tomatoes and pureed anchos, raise the heat to high, and bring the mixture to a boil. Reduce the heat to medium and simmer for 25 minutes.

2. Puree in a blender or processor, or in the pan and using a hand-held blender. Season to taste with salt and pepper and whisk in the crème fraîche. *May be prepared up to 2 days ahead and refrigerated.* Reheat, stirring, over low heat just before serving.

Makes 1¼ cups

[Photograph on page 98

fish & shellfish

Pan-fried Red Snapper in Blue Cornmeal

Served with Southwestern Fries (page 151), this is a Southwestern fish and chips. The fish is very lightly coated in blue cornmeal and pan-fried, not deep-fried. Serve it with Green Chile Aioli.

4 large eggs, lightly beaten
Salt and freshly ground pepper
2 cups seasoned all-purpose flour
    (page 6)
2 cups seasoned blue cornmeal
    (page 6)
6 red snapper fillets
    (about 6 ounces each)
½ cup olive oil
½ cup Smoked Red Pepper Sauce
    (page 64)
6 tablespoons Green Chile Aioli, or
    6 tablespoons Papaya-Tomatillo Salsa to
    taste (page 134)

1. Season the eggs lightly with salt and pepper. Place the eggs, flour, and cornmeal in 3 separate bowls. Season the snapper fillets lightly on both sides with salt and pepper.

2. In a large sauté pan over medium-high heat, heat the oil. Dredge each fillet in the flour and shake off any excess. Dip into the beaten egg and let the excess drip off.

3. Sauté for 3 minutes on each side and drizzle with the red pepper sauce. Serve immediately, garnished with Green Chile Aioli.

Makes 6 servings

Green Chile Aioli

1 cup good-quality mayonnaise
1 teaspoon minced fresh garlic
1 poblano, roasted, peeled, and seeded
    (page 8)
2 tablespoons fresh lime juice
Salt and freshly ground pepper

Combine the mayonnaise, garlic, poblano, lime juice, and salt and pepper to taste in a food processor and process until the poblano is pureed. *May be prepared up to 1 day ahead, covered, and refrigerated.* Bring to room temperature before serving.

Makes about 1 cup

Red Snapper Roasted in Banana Leaves
with Red Curry Sauce

In Mexico and in the American Southwest, banana leaves are often used as a wrapper for cooking fish or tamales. Like corn husks, they keep the flavors in and impart a subtle but distinct aroma of their own. If you can't get banana leaves, wrap the fish in parchment paper.

> 4 red snapper fillets (6 ounces each)
> 4 teaspoons olive oil
> Salt and freshly ground black pepper
> 2 banana leaves, each cut in half
>   (page 5)
> 1 cup Red Curry Sauce

1. Preheat the oven to 400° F.

2. Rub each fillet with 1 teaspoon olive oil, season to taste with salt and pepper, and wrap, envelope style, in half a banana leaf. Place, seam side down, in an oiled baking pan and roast for 7 minutes.

3. Place each portion of fish on a plate, seam side up, and open the packet. Serve on the banana leaf, topped with about 4 tablespoons of curry sauce. Serve extra sauce in a bowl in the center of the table.

Makes 4 servings

Red Curry Sauce

> 2 tablespoons unsalted butter
> 2 tablespoons coarsely chopped
>   fresh ginger
> 1 tablespoon chopped garlic
> 2 tablespoons chopped white onion
> 1 cup white wine
> 1 cup Fish Stock (page 16)
> 1½ cups heavy cream
> 1 tablespoon red curry paste (page 6)
> ½ roasted red bell pepper, peeled and
>   seeded (page 8)
> ½ teaspoon sugar
> Salt and freshly ground pepper

1. In a medium saucepan over medium heat, melt the butter and sweat the ginger, garlic, and onion for 3 minutes. Raise the heat to high, add the wine and stock, and reduce until 2 tablespoons of liquid remain. Reduce the heat to medium, add the cream, and simmer for 10 minutes. Whisk in the red curry paste and simmer for 10 minutes more.

2. In a blender, combine the sauce and the roasted pepper and process until smooth. Strain through a fine strainer into a bowl, add the sugar and salt and pepper to taste, and mix well. *May be prepared up to 1 day in advance, covered, and refrigerated.* Bring to room temperature before serving.

Makes about 1 cup

Pan-fried Red Snapper

with Warm Tomato Relish

For this dish you sauté the snapper and put it on the plate. Then you quickly deglaze the pan with Tomato Relish. The juices from the fish go into the relish and back on the plate.

2 cups Tomato Relish
6 fillets Pan-fried Red Snapper (page 94)

1. Prepare the relish and set aside.
2. Cook the fillets and remove to a warm plate. Return the skillet to the heat and pour the relish into the skillet. Deglaze for about 15 seconds over high heat.
3. To serve, spoon some of the relish over each fillet.
Makes 6 servings

Tomato Relish

1 medium tomato, coarsely chopped
2 tablespoons finely diced red onion
1 cup chopped scallions
3 tablespoons basil chiffonnade
1 tablespoon minced garlic
1 tablespoon balsamic vinegar
2 tablespoons olive oil
Salt and freshly ground pepper

Combine the tomato, onion, scallions, basil, garlic, vinegar, and oil. Season to taste with salt and pepper. *May be prepared up to 1 day ahead, covered, and refrigerated.* Bring to room temperature before serving.
Makes 2 cups

Pan-fried Red Snapper with Tomato–New Mexico Red Chile Sauce, recipe page 94–95

Yucatán-style Mako Shark

with Avocado-Tomato Salsa

Mako shark is a good alternative to swordfish, with a similar texture and slightly gamier flavor. It is hearty enough to hold up to this spicy marinade.

4 mako shark steaks (about
   6 ounces each)
3 tablespoons Yucatán Marinade
8 Tablespoons Avocado-Tomato Salsa, or
   to taste (page 76)

1. About 1 hour before grilling, brush the fish steaks on both sides with the marinade, cover, and refrigerate.

2. Prepare a wood or charcoal fire and let it burn down to embers, or preheat the broiler.

3. Grill the steaks for 3 minutes on each side, until medium. Serve topped with 2 tablespoons salsa.

Makes 4 servings

Yucatán Marinade

¼ cup fresh orange juice
¼ cup fresh lime juice
2 tablespoons fresh lemon juice
¼ cup ancho chile powder
2 tablespoons pasilla chile powder
¼ cup paprika
1 teaspoon cayenne
1 teaspoon freshly ground black pepper
1 teaspoon salt
¼ cup olive oil

   In a food processor, combine all the ingredients except the olive oil and process for 30 seconds. With the motor running, slowly add the olive oil and process until emulsified. *May be prepared up to 1 day ahead, covered, and refrigerated.*

Makes 1 cup

Pan-roasted Whole Fish

Fish stays moister when it is cooked on the bone, and this crisp, juicy fish is well worth the slight extra bother of deboning at the table. Use baby red snapper or baby black sea bass, with the heads cut off, if you prefer.

6 whole fish (about 1 pound each)
Salt and freshly ground pepper
½ cup olive oil
2 tablespoons unsalted butter
1½ cups Charred Jalapeño-Basil
   Vinaigrette (page 94)

1. Preheat the oven to 400° F.

2. Make 4 diagonal cuts on each side of each fish, making sure to reach all the way down to the bone. Season the fish with salt and pepper to taste on both sides.

3. In a large sauté pan over medium-high heat, heat the olive oil until it begins to smoke. Place the fish in the pan and sear on 1 side. Add the butter and let the fish brown, about 3 minutes. Turn the fish over, transfer to the oven, and cook until done, 5 to 7 minutes longer, depending on the size and density of the fish.

4. Transfer each fish to a plate and ladle the vinaigrette over the fish.

Makes 6 servings

Roasted Lobster

Roasting lobsters is as simple as roasting any other fish or shellfish. Just be careful not to overcook. Because lobster has such great texture, it goes well with complex sauces like the Smoked Tomato–Lobster Sauce.

4 lobsters (1½ pounds each)
½ cup olive oil
Salt and freshly ground pepper

1. Preheat the oven to 350° F.

2. Make a small incision right down the middle of each live lobster and split it open to expose the meat. (You can break the shell with your hands.) Brush it with olive oil.

3. Place the lobster on a baking sheet, shell side down, brush with olive oil, and roast for 12 to 15 minutes, or until cooked. Serve immediately.

Makes 4 servings

Smoked Tomato–Lobster Sauce

Serve roasted lobsters out of the shell topped with this sauce.

½ tablespoon unsalted butter
¼ cup finely chopped celery
¼ cup finely chopped carrot
¼ cup finely chopped onion
¾ cup white wine
1 cup Lobster Stock (page 17)
½ cup heavy cream
¾ cup chopped cold-smoked tomatoes (page 7)
Salt and freshly ground pepper

1. In a large saucepan over medium heat, melt the butter and sweat the celery, carrot, and onion. Add the wine, raise the heat to high, and reduce the wine completely. Add the stock and reduce by a third. Remove from the heat and strain. *May be prepared up to 2 days ahead, covered, and refrigerated.*

2. Meanwhile, cook the cream over high heat until reduced by half.

3. Return the sauce to high heat, whisk in the cream, and bring to a boil. Add the tomatoes, and puree in a blender or processor, or in the pan with a hand-held blender. Season to taste with salt and pepper.

Makes 3 cups

Roasted Lobster on Blue Corn Pancakes

with Red Curry Sauce & Corn Relish

You can eat this appetizer with a knife and fork, or if you want, wrap the lobster, curry sauce, and relish in the pancake and pick it up with your fingers.

2 lobsters (1½ pounds each)
2 tablespoons unsalted butter,
  melted (optional)
4 Blue Corn Pancakes (page 86)
1 cup Corn Relish
1 cup Red Curry Sauce (page 97)

1. Roast the lobsters as described on page 102 and remove the meat from the shell. Or cook the lobsters for 5 minutes in boiling water to cover and take the meat out of the shell. *May be done 3 hours ahead, covered, and refrigerated.* If prepared ahead, brush with melted butter and put into a pre-heated 350° F. oven for 5 minutes or heat the butter in a skillet over medium heat and add the lobster. Sear it on one side, turn it over, and cook for about 3 minutes, just until cooked through. Then proceed.

2. Prepare the pancakes and set aside.

3. To serve, place the warm corn pancakes on a serving platter or individual plates. Top each with a layer of warm lobster and a layer of relish. Garnish with the curry sauce.

Makes 4 first-course servings

Roasted Lobster on Blue Corn Pancakes with Red Curry Sauce & Corn Relish, right

Corn Relish

2 cups roasted corn kernels (page 8)
3 tablespoons finely diced red onion
2 tablespoons minced jalapeño
¼ cup coarsely chopped cilantro
¼ cup fresh lime juice
2 tablespoons finely diced roasted red
  bell pepper (page 8)
2 tablespoons olive oil
Salt and freshly ground pepper

Combine the corn, onion, jalapeño, cilantro, lime juice, red pepper, and olive oil in a bowl. Season to taste with salt and pepper. *May be prepared up to 6 hours ahead, covered, and refrigerated.* Bring to room temperature before serving.

Makes about 2 cups

Grilled Shrimp

Shrimp go well with bold flavors because their own flavor is neutral. Grill them very quickly to preserve their splendid texture and serve with Green Curry Sauce, Garlic and Red Chile Oil (page 106), or Red Chile Pesto (page 106).

20 large shrimp, shelled and deveined (about 1¼ pounds)
5 tablespoons olive oil
Salt and freshly ground pepper

1. Prepare a wood or charcoal fire and let it burn down to embers, or preheat the broiler.

2. Rub the shrimp with olive oil and season to taste with salt and pepper. Grill or broil for 2½ minutes on each side. Serve immediately.
Makes 4 servings

[Grilled Shrimp with Garlic and Red Chile Oil

Green Curry Sauce

Top grilled shrimp with this fiery curry sauce.
2 tablespoons unsalted butter
2 tablespoons coarsely chopped ginger
2 tablespoons coarsely chopped onion
2 tablespoons coarsely chopped garlic
1 cup white wine
1½ cups coconut milk (page 5)
2 tablespoons green curry paste (page 6)
1 cup Fish or Lobster Stock (pages 16–17)
1½ cups heavy cream
½ cup (packed) fresh spinach leaves
½ teaspoon sugar
Salt and freshly ground pepper

1. In a large saucepan over medium heat, melt the butter and sweat the ginger, onion, and garlic for 3 minutes. Raise the heat to high, add the wine, bring to a boil, and reduce until 2 tablespoons of liquid remain. Add the coconut milk and green curry paste and boil until the coconut milk is reduced by half. Add the stock and reduce by three-fourths. Add the cream and bring to a boil. Reduce the heat to medium and simmer for 10 minutes.

2. In a blender, combine the sauce and spinach and blend for 30 seconds. Strain the sauce, add the sugar, and season to taste with salt and pepper. *May be made up to 2 days ahead, covered, and refrigerated.* Reheat, stirring, just before serving.
Makes 1½ cups

Red Chile
Pesto

½ cup shelled pumpkin seeds
2 tablespoons fresh lime juice
2 tablespoons minced garlic
½ cup Ancho Puree (page 8)
½ cup olive oil
Salt and freshly ground pepper

In a food processor, combine the pumpkin seeds, lime juice, garlic, and ancho puree and process until well mixed. With the motor running, slowly add the olive oil until emulsified. Season to taste with salt and pepper. *May be prepared up to 2 days ahead, covered, and refrigerated.* Bring to room temperature before serving.
Makes about 1 cup

Garlic &
Red Chile Oil

Shrimp with garlic is a well-known Spanish dish and is part of the tapas menu. Here, this oil adds hints of the Southwest. Serve the shrimp alone with the oil poured over or with flour tortillas that have been briefly heated in the oven.

1 cup plus 1 tablespoon olive oil
2 tablespoons minced garlic
1 tablespoon chopped fresh thyme leaves
 or 1 teaspoon dried
1 tablespoon chopped fresh rosemary leaves
 or 1 teaspoon dried
2 chipotles
1 teaspoon ancho chile powder
2 tablespoons fresh lime juice
Salt and freshly ground pepper

In a small skillet over medium heat, heat 1 tablespoon of the olive oil and sauté the garlic just until softened. Put the garlic, thyme, rosemary, chipotles, chile powder, and lime juice in a blender and process until smooth. Add the remaining 1 cup of oil and blend for 2 minutes. Season to taste with salt and pepper. *May be made up to 1 day ahead and refrigerated, covered.* Reheat, stirring, just before serving.
Makes 1½ cups

Grilled Sea Scallops

Use the biggest sea scallops you can find so they will stay moist when grilled. Don't let them overcook—they should be a touch raw inside or they'll turn into little hockey pucks. Tomato-Cumin Sauce is an excellent choice to serve with perfectly grilled scallops.

20 large sea scallops (about 12 ounces)
5 tablespoons olive oil
Salt and freshly ground black pepper

1. Prepare a wood or charcoal fire and let it burn down to embers, or preheat the broiler.

2. Rub the scallops with olive oil and season to taste with salt and pepper. Grill or broil 2½ minutes on each side. Serve immediately.

Makes 4 servings

Tomato-Cumin Sauce

1 tablespoon unsalted butter
2 tablespoons finely chopped red onion
1 tablespoon finely chopped garlic
One 8-ounce can whole tomatoes, seeded and drained
1 teaspoon pasilla chile powder
1 teaspoon ancho chile powder
1 teaspoon ground toasted cumin seeds (page 9)
Salt and freshly ground pepper
Honey
3 tablespoons crème fraîche (page 6)

In a large saucepan over medium heat, melt the butter and sweat the onion and garlic. Add the tomatoes, chile powders, and cumin and simmer for 45 minutes. Puree the mixture in a blender or food processor, or in the pot with a hand-held blender until smooth. Season to taste with salt, pepper, and honey. *May be made up to 2 days ahead and refrigerated, covered.* Fold in the crème fraîche and reheat, stirring, just before serving.

Makes 1 cup

Grilled Sea Scallops with Avocado-Corn Relish on Crisp Tortillas

The great thing here is not only the flavor but the mix of textures—the crispness of the tortilla, the crunchiness of the corn, and the creaminess of the avocado, all accenting the sweet, juicy scallops.

2 cups peanut oil
4 flour tortillas, cut into quarters
16 large sea scallops, grilled (page 107)
6 tablespoons Avocado-Corn Relish

1. In a large saucepan or deep fryer over medium-high heat, heat the oil to 375° F., or until a piece of tortilla sizzles when immersed. Fry the tortillas until crisp and drain on paper towels. Set aside.

2. Grill the scallops as described on page 107.

3. To serve, arrange 4 tortilla quarters on each plate. Top each with a layer of relish and 1 scallop.
Makes 4 first-course servings

Avocado-Corn Relish

2 Haas avocados, peeled, seeded, and
    coarsely chopped
1 cup roasted corn kernels (page 8)
3 tablespoons finely diced red onion
¼ cup coarsely chopped cilantro
¼ cup fresh lime juice
2 tablespoons regular or light sour cream
Salt and freshly ground pepper

Combine the avocados, corn, onion, cilantro, lime juice, and sour cream in a bowl and mix well. Season to taste with salt and pepper. *May be prepared up to 1 day ahead, covered, and refrigerated. Bring to room temperature before serving.*
Makes 2½ cups

Cornmeal-coated Oysters

This dish has become a favorite at Mesa Grill. People can't figure out that the mysterious, haunting flavor in the cornmeal is curry.

    20 oysters
    2 cups fine yellow cornmeal
    1 tablespoon cayenne
    1 tablespoon Curry Powder (page 6)
    1 tablespoon salt
    1 tablespoon freshly ground pepper
    1 small head radicchio, shredded
    ½ cup Whole-Grain Mustard Sauce
    1 cup olive oil

1. Shuck the oysters, reserving the best 20 half shells.

2. Mix the cornmeal with the cayenne, curry powder, salt, and pepper. Divide the radicchio among 4 plates and place 5 oyster shells on each plate, held steady by the radicchio. Put 1 teaspoon mustard sauce in each shell.

3. In a small sauté pan over medium heat, heat the olive oil. For each serving, coat 5 oysters at a time in the cornmeal mixture and sauté for about 45 seconds on each side. Place 1 cooked oyster in each shell and serve immediately with the sauce.

Makes 4 first-course servings

Whole-grain Mustard Sauce

½ tablespoon unsalted butter
1½ teaspoons coarsely chopped red onion
¾ teaspoon minced garlic
¼ cup white wine
½ cup heavy cream
1¼ tablespoons whole-grain mustard
1½ teaspoons coarsely chopped cilantro
Salt and freshly ground pepper

In a medium saucepan over medium heat, melt the butter and sweat the onion and garlic for 3 minutes. Raise the heat to high, add the wine, and reduce to three-fourths. Add the heavy cream and bring to a boil. Reduce the heat to medium and simmer for 10 minutes. Remove from the heat, and add the mustard and cilantro. Season to taste with salt and pepper. *May be made up to 2 days ahead, covered, and refrigerated.* Reheat, stirring, just before serving.

Makes about ½ cup

Southwestern Ceviche

Jonathan Waxman inspired this colorful dish. Using several different kinds of fish, as well as fruit and jalapeños, adds dimension. The fish must be marinated in fresh lime juice—bottled juice won't work.

- ¾ pound medium shrimp, shelled and deveined
- ¾ pound sea scallops, cut in ½-inch dice
- ¾ pound salmon fillet, cut in ½-inch dice
- 1 cup diced tomatoes (½-inch dice)
- 1 cup diced mango (½-inch dice)
- ½ cup diced red onion (½-inch dice)
- 2 jalapeños, minced
- 4 cups fresh lime juice
- 1 cup chopped cilantro
- 2 tablespoons sugar
- Salt and freshly ground pepper
- 2 grapefruits, peeled and segmented
- 3 oranges, peeled and segmented
- 4 limes, peeled and segmented

1. Parboil the shrimp in water to cover for 3 minutes, then drain. Cut into ½-inch dice.

2. In a large nonreactive mixing bowl, combine the scallops, salmon, shrimp, tomatoes, mango, onion, jalapeño, and lime juice. Marinate, refrigerated, for 2½ to 3 hours.

3. Just before serving, drain off as much lime juice as possible and add the cilantro, sugar, and salt and pepper to taste. Gently mix in the grapefruit, orange, and lime sections, being careful not to break them up.

Makes 6 to 8 servings

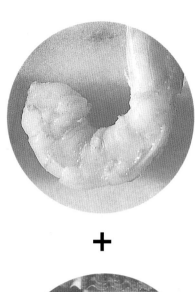

+

+

meat, poultry, + game

don't worry, the

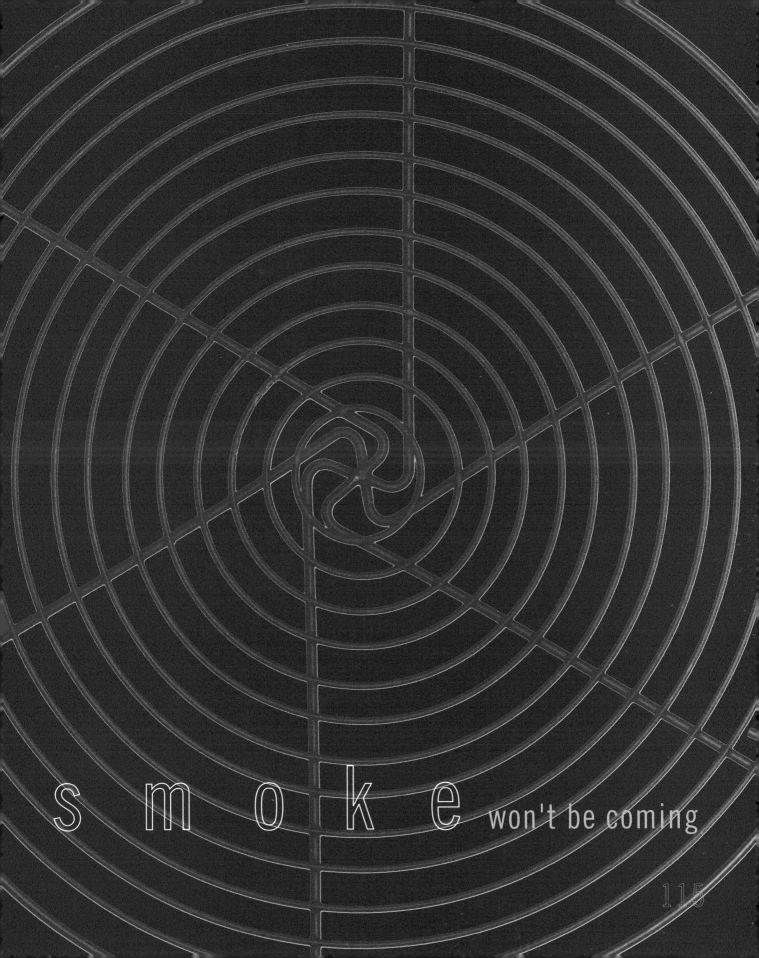

smoke won't be coming

out of your   all the rich flavors stand out

t he concept of meat as a condiment isn't for me. Using small amounts of meat to season other foods won't work for Southwest American cooking. All the meat dishes I prepare are the hefty center of a meal, whether they are based on beef, veal, lamb, pork, or poultry. Some are Southwestern in origin, but many come from other cuisines and are given American makeovers with chiles, herbs, and cornmeal.

Steak with Southwestern Fries and Red Chile Mustard, with its fruity anchos, sharp mustard, and fiery potatoes, is my interpretation of the French bistro dish, *steak frites*. In other updates of steak classics, a compound butter with smoky chipotle flavor melts into a pan-seared steak and provides a fragrant sauce; filet mignon, coated with red chiles and seared, has its peppery aura intensified with a wild mushroom and ancho chile sauce. And I can't resist giving my signature to Italian osso buco with smoked tomatoes and some well-chosen chiles. Don't worry, the smoke won't be coming out of your ears. All the rich flavors stand out, not just the chiles.

Lamb is one of my favorite meats, and it really belongs on a Southwestern menu. Coat it with a red chile marinade before roasting, and the marinade turns into a dark red crust in the oven. You can make an unusual chili out of leg of lamb and black

beans—one that has a stronger flavor than the traditional beef chilies—and serve it with Avocado Relish. Of course, lamb chops are everyone's favorite home-style dish, and mine sizzle in a shiny puddle of Jalapeño Preserves.

Pork is another natural on the Southwestern table. I like to marinate the tenderloin in chipotles and grill it, then serve it with a tart Green Apple Juice Sauce. Smoking the loin and grilling slices to serve with an Apricot–Serrano Chile Sauce creates a dish that sings high, low, loud, and soft, all at the same time. I treat pork chops with adobo, a marinade they can handle, and trade in their traditional applesauce for a Spicy Apple Chutney. Barbecued ribs slowly cooked in the oven my way are tender and flavorful under a smooth yet smoky-hot Peanut-Chipotle Sauce with the kick of ginger.

Venison has a strong flavor and is low in fat and calories. I cut it into medallions and pan-roast it quickly to be sure it stays tender, then serve with a Spicy Black Grape Sauce that has the intensity venison craves.

In my kitchen, chicken, duck, and other birds are paired with lively chiles and piquant and fruity salsas and relishes. When you stuff a chicken with sage and garlic and roast it in Red Chile Oil, you end up with a whole range of herbal, spicy flavors. Marinate chicken breasts, as I do, with a ginger and garlic marinade, grill it, and serve them with a summery corn and grilled pepper relish. I also like to use a Yucatán Marinade that combines citrus and chiles, especially for chicken thighs and legs, and repeat those notes in a Papaya-Tomatillo Salsa. Try slow-cooked duck Asian style in a complex barbecue sauce, then serve the breast meat with a crunchy Pineapple–Red Onion Relish. The combination of meltingly rich (and surprisingly mild) roasted duck and the fresh relish flavors makes beautiful music. And finally, move your traditional Thanksgiving table to the American Southwest, with Pan-roasted Squab, Blue Corn–Chorizo Dressing, and a spicy-tart cranberry relish.

Pan-roasted Squab

with Blue Corn– Chorizo Dressing & Cranberry-Mango Relish

Squab are farm-raised pigeons that weigh about a pound each. Fresh squab—the best kind—is available at many butchers and supermarkets, but you can make do with frozen.

4 tablespoons unsalted butter
6 squab (about 1 pound each)
Salt and freshly ground black pepper
1 recipe Blue Corn–Chorizo Stuffing
2 cups Cranberry-Mango Relish

1. Preheat the oven to 450° F.

2. In a roasting pan, melt the butter. Place the squab, breast side down, in the pan and roast for 12 to 14 minutes. Remove from the oven and let rest for 5 minutes.

3. Fill the squab with the dressing and serve with the relish.
   Makes 6 servings

Blue Corn– Chorizo Dressing

½ cup unsalted butter
1 pound chorizo, finely diced
6 garlic cloves, finely diced
¼ cup finely diced celery
1 medium onion, finely diced
¼ cup finely diced carrot
1 poblano, finely diced
1 recipe Blue Cornbread, crumbled (page 167)
1 teaspoon coarsely chopped thyme leaves
1 teaspoon coarsely chopped sage leaves
1 tablespoon coarsely chopped cilantro
½ cup Chicken Stock (page 16) or water
Salt and freshly ground black pepper

1. Preheat the oven to 350° F.

2. In a medium sauté pan over medium heat, melt the butter and cook the chorizo, garlic, celery, onion, carrot, and poblano for 3 minutes, or until lightly browned.

3. Transfer to a mixing bowl and add the cornbread, thyme, sage, cilantro, and stock, and mix well. *May be prepared up to 2 days ahead and refrigerated.* Place in a 12 x 15-inch baking pan and bake for 25 minutes.
   Makes 6 servings

Cranberry- Mango Relish

Very much a fall item, this beautiful red-and-yellow relish goes well with roasted duck or game birds.

1 cup fresh cranberries, simmered in water
**   to cover until they pop, about 10 minutes**
1 large mango, peeled, seeded, and coarsely
**   chopped (page 7)**
3 tablespoons finely diced red onion
1 tablespoon minced jalapeño
¼ cup coarsely chopped cilantro
¼ cup fresh lime juice
2 tablespoons sugar
Salt and freshly ground pepper

Combine the cranberries, mango, onion, jalapeño, cilantro, lime juice, and sugar in a bowl and season to taste with salt and pepper. *Refrigerate, covered, for up to 1 day.* Bring to room temperature before serving.
Makes about 2½ cups

Red Chile–crusted Filet Mignon

with Wild Mushroom– Ancho Chile Sauce

This rich, chunky dish is kind of like the old steak au poivre. Serve it with the rich, chunky mushroom sauce and Black Bean–Goat Cheese Tortas (page 158).

6 New Mexico red chiles
1 tablespoon black peppercorns
4 tablespoons oil
4 filet mignon steaks
   (about 8 ounces each)

1. Preheat the oven to 300° F.

2. Spread out the chiles on a baking sheet and roast for about 30 seconds. Remove the seeds and stems, place the flesh in a food processor, and chop coarsely. In a coffee grinder, grind the peppercorns to about the same consistency as the chiles. Mix the two and reserve in a pie pan.

3. In a large sauté pan over high heat, heat the oil until it begins to smoke. Dredge each steak on 1 side in the pepper mixture and cook, pepper side down, for 1 minute, or until brown and crisp. Turn the meat over, reduce the heat to medium, and cook for 3 to 4 minutes more, until done to your liking.

4. Serve with the mushroom sauce. Spoon a little sauce over each steak and pass the rest in a bowl.

Makes 4 servings

Wild Mushroom– Ancho Chile Sauce

2 tablespoons unsalted butter
½ medium red onion, diced
2 tablespoons finely chopped garlic
2 cups red wine
½ pound shiitake mushrooms, stems
   removed and caps sliced ¼ inch thick
½ pound cremini mushrooms, stems
   removed and caps sliced ¼ inch thick
½ pound portobello mushrooms, stems
   removed and caps sliced ¼ inch thick
3½ cups Chicken Stock (page 16)
¾ cup Ancho Puree (page 8)
2 tablespoons honey
Salt and freshly ground pepper

1. In a large saucepan over medium heat, melt the butter and sweat the onion and garlic for about 3 minutes. Raise the heat to high, add the wine, and boil 10 minutes, until reduced to dry. Reduce the heat to medium, add the mushrooms, cook until soft, and add the stock. Raise the heat to high and bring the mixture to a boil. Reduce the heat to medium and simmer for 15 minutes.

2. Whisk in the ancho puree and cook for 5 minutes more. Add the honey and salt and pepper to taste. Keep hot in a double boiler until ready to serve. *May be made up to 2 days ahead and refrigerated.* Reheat, stirring, just before serving.

Makes 4 cups

Loin Lamb Chops
with Jalapeño Preserves

Lamb chops with mint jelly was one of my mother's favorite combinations, and it was often on the table when I came home late for dinner. She may have given up waiting for me, but the lamb chops were still there. Jalapeño Preserves are a lot livelier than mint jelly; they wake up the simply grilled chops.

8 loin lamb chops
3 tablespoons olive oil
Salt and freshly ground black pepper
½ cup Jalapeño Preserves

1. Prepare a wood or charcoal fire and let it burn down to embers, or preheat the broiler.

2. Brush the chops lightly with oil, season to taste with salt and pepper, and grill or broil 4 minutes per side for medium rare, or to your liking.

3. Bring the preserves to room temperature and serve with the lamb chops, allowing about 2 tablespoons per serving.

Makes 4 servings

Jalapeño
Preserves

These preserves are also good with roast lamb. Try them on warm Blue Cornbread (page 167) spread with a little butter for a real treat. Do not multiply or divide this recipe; it won't work.

3 medium red bell peppers, seeded and
    coarsely chopped
6 jalapeños, minced
4 cups sugar
1¼ cups red wine vinegar
¾ cup liquid fruit pectin

1. In a heavy 2-quart saucepan over high heat, combine the peppers, jalapeños, sugar, and vinegar and bring to a boil. Reduce the heat to medium and simmer for 20 minutes, stirring every 5 minutes. Be careful not to let the mixture boil over.

2. Turn off the heat and add the pectin, mixing well. Turn the heat on again to high and cook until the mixture comes back to a boil. Pour into sterilized jars and seal according to the manufacturer's directions. *May also be refrigerated, covered, for up to 6 months in a nonreactive bowl or jar.*

Makes 6 cups

Chipotle Pork Tenderloin

with Green Apple Juice Sauce

I like to rework classic combinations in novel ways, to sort of make them my own. Pork and apples is one such classic, and here it takes the form of smoky pork tenderloin, punched up by chipotles and moistened with a Green Apple Juice Sauce. Serve the meat with Spicy Apple Chutney (page 131) and Baked Sweet Potato Tamales with Orange-Honey Butter (page 32).

2½ pounds pork tenderloin
½ cup pureed canned chipotles
1 cup Green Apple Juice Sauce

1. Rub the tenderloins with the pureed chipotles, cover, and refrigerate for at least 2 hours or overnight.

2. Prepare a wood or charcoal fire and let it burn down to embers, or preheat the broiler.

3. Grill the tenderloins for 10 to 12 minutes, turning. Slice very thin and pour the sauce over the meat.

Makes 6 servings

Green Apple Juice Sauce

2 tablespoons unsalted butter
2 jalapeños, coarsely chopped
1 medium onion, coarsely chopped
2 cups Chicken Stock (page 16)
1½ cups frozen green apple juice concentrate (12-ounce can)
3 tablespoons light brown sugar
Salt and freshly ground pepper

In a medium saucepan over medium-high heat, melt the butter and sweat the jalapeños and onion. Add the stock, apple juice concentrate, and brown sugar and cook until reduced by half, about 30 minutes. Season to taste with salt and pepper. *May be made up to 2 days ahead and refrigerated, covered.* Reheat, stirring, just before serving.

Makes 1 cup

Barbecued Ribs
with Peanut-Chipotle Sauce

These ribs are baked slowly, rather than grilled, and they become really tender. The combination of peanuts and chipotles smoothes the sharp edges of the barbecue sauce.

> 1 cup soy sauce
> 4 tablespoons coarsely chopped ginger
> 2 racks of pork ribs (12 ribs each)
> 2½ cups Peanut-Chipotle Sauce
> 2½ cups Corn-Tomatillo Salsa
> 2 cups chopped peanuts

1. Preheat the oven to 400° F.

2. In a saucepan over medium-high heat, combine the soy sauce, 2 cups of water, and the ginger and bring to a boil. Pour the mixture into the bottom of a roasting pan and place the ribs on a rack in the pan. Brush with the Peanut-Chipotle Sauce.

3. Place in the oven and bake for 1¼ hours, basting every 10 minutes. Remove from the oven and cut into single ribs. Stack or arrange them on plates, accompanied by the salsa. Just before serving, sprinkle with peanuts.

Makes 4 servings

Tracie made these great but needed more browning

Peanut-Chipotle Sauce

delish

> 1½ cups New Mexico–style Barbecue Sauce (page 36)
> ½ cup smooth peanut butter
> ¼ cup soy sauce
> 1½ tablespoons rice wine vinegar
> 1½ teaspoons pureed canned chipotles
> 1½ tablespoons honey

Combine the barbecue sauce, peanut butter, soy sauce, vinegar, pureed chipotles, and the honey. Mix well and reserve. *May be made up to 4 days ahead and refrigerated, covered.*

Makes about 2½ cups

Corn-Tomatillo Salsa

great

> 1 cup roasted corn kernels (page 8)
> 2 medium tomatillos, husked and coarsely chopped
> 1 tablespoon finely diced red onion
> 1½ teaspoons minced jalapeño
> 2 tablespoons fresh lime juice
> 2 tablespoons coarsely chopped cilantro
> ½ teaspoon honey
> Salt and freshly ground pepper

Combine the corn, tomatillos, onion, jalapeño, lime juice, cilantro, and honey in a bowl and season to taste with salt and pepper. *Refrigerate, covered, for up to 1 day.* Bring to room temperature 1 hour before serving.

Makes about 2½ cups

use more of everything

Lamb & Black Bean Chili with Avocado Relish

Lamb makes a rich, delicious chili. I'm not sure what the rules are about chili—some people say you should have beans in it and some people consider them to be just filler. Personally, I think beans round out the dish; without them, you would just have meat cooked in sauce.

> 2½ pounds lamb from the leg, boned
>   and cut into ½ inch cubes
> 1 cup olive oil
> 1½ large onions, finely diced
> 1½ tablespoons chopped garlic
> ¾ cup dark beer
> One 16-ounce can whole tomatoes,
>   drained and pureed
> 1½ pureed canned chipotles
> ¾ cup ancho chile powder
> ½ cup pasilla chile powder
> 1 tablespoon ground cumin
> 2 cups Chicken Stock (page 16)
> 3 cups cooked or canned black beans, drained
> 6 tablespoons fresh lime juice
> Salt and freshly ground black pepper
> ¾ cup Avocado Relish, or to taste (page 38)

1. In a large frying pan over high heat, heat the oil until it begins to smoke. Add the cubed lamb and sauté until seared and brown on all sides. Add the onions and garlic and cook for 3 minutes, taking care not to let them burn. Add the beer and reduce until it has completely evaporated. Add the tomatoes, chipotles, chile powders, and cumin. Stir well and cook for 10 minutes.

2. Reduce the heat to medium, add the stock, and simmer for 45 minutes. Add the beans and simmer for 15 minutes more. Degrease. Add the lime juice and salt and pepper to taste. Transfer to a serving dish and serve hot with the salsa on the side. *May be made up to 2 days ahead and refrigerated, covered. Reheat, stirring, just before serving.*
   Makes 8 servings

Grilled New York Steak with Red Chile Mustard

A well-grilled steak is always appreciated; it becomes extra special when it gets a blast of chile mustard. Serve the steak with Southwestern Fries (page 15) and Thyme-marinated Tomatoes (page 144).

> 6 New York strip steaks (10 ounces each)
> 1½ cups Red Chile Mustard

1. Prepare a wood or charcoal fire and let it burn down to embers, or preheat the broiler.

2. Grill the steaks until done to your liking, about 4 minutes on each side for medium rare. Serve with chile mustard to taste.
   Makes 6 servings

Red Chile Mustard

You may not be able to identify the chile in this sauce, but you'll know it's there.
2 cups Dijon mustard
3 tablespoons ancho chile powder
   Combine the mustard, ancho chile powder, and 3 tablespoons lukewarm water and mix well. *May be prepared up to 1 week ahead and refrigerated.* Bring to room temperature before serving.
Makes 2 cups

Pan-seared
New York Steak
with Chipotle Butter

This time, instead of being grilled, the steaks are cooked in a cast-iron skillet over high heat. (You may want to use two skillets.) Searing in a little olive oil gives them a crisp crust that retains all the juices of the meat. Do the steaks two at a time (in each pan) and let rest until serving. Steaks can also be charcoal grilled as directed on page 124. Serve with Twice-baked Potatoes (page 148) and a salad of mixed greens.

6 New York strip steaks (10 ounces each)
2 tablespoons ground cumin
Salt and freshly ground pepper
½ cup olive oil
¾ cup Chipotle Butter

1. Season the steaks with cumin and salt and pepper to taste. Set aside.

2. In a large cast-iron skillet over high heat, heat the olive oil until it begins to smoke. Add the steaks and sear on 1 side for about 4 minutes. Turn and cook on the other side for about 4 minutes for medium-rare.

3. Remove the steaks from the pan and place on individual plates. Cut six ½-inch-thick slices of compound butter from the log and place one on top of each steak. Serve immediately.

Makes 6 servings

Chipotle Butter

8 tablespoons (1 stick) unsalted butter
1 canned chipotle, stemmed
1 garlic clove
2 tablespoons chopped red onion
Salt and freshly ground pepper

In a food processor, combine the butter, chipotle, garlic, onion, and salt and pepper to taste. Process until completely mixed. Spread the butter in a cylinder about 1 inch in diameter along the long side of a sheet of parchment paper or wax paper, leaving a 1-inch border. Roll up the butter in the paper to make a log. Refrigerate for at least 30 minutes. *May be refrigerated for up to 3 days or frozen.*

Makes 1 cup

Veal Shanks

with Smoked Tomatoes & Queso Fresco

Veal shanks used to be really inexpensive; sometimes you could even get them for free at the butcher, because no one wanted to buy them. Then osso buco became popular and turned veal shanks into designer food. They cost more now, but they're worth it. My rendition of the Italian classic is good winter food and one of the few slow-cooking dishes that I do. Although the method of cooking is traditional, smoked tomatoes and queso fresco give it Southwestern flavor and style. You can serve the veal with Cilantro Risotto Cakes (page 151) and fresh sautéed spinach.

1½ cups olive oil
6 pieces veal shank cut for osso buco
    (about 1 pound each)
1 cup seasoned flour (page 6)
2 medium carrots, coarsely diced
2 medium onions, coarsely diced
2 celery stalks, coarsely diced
8 medium tomatoes, cold-smoked (page 7)
2 cups red wine
1 cup veal stock or Chicken
    Stock (page 16)
4 roasted garlic cloves (page 8)
1 tablespoon pureed canned chipotles
Zest of 2 lemons, grated
3 tablespoons ancho chile powder
2 tablespoons honey
Salt and freshly ground pepper
½ cup fresh lemon juice
½ pound queso fresco or Monterey Jack

1. Preheat the oven to 400° F.

2. In a very large skillet or roasting pan over high heat, heat the oil until smoking. Dredge the veal in the seasoned flour on 1 side and sear that side until browned.

3. Turn the veal over and add the carrots, onions, celery, smoked tomatoes, wine, stock, and garlic. Place in the oven and cook, covered, for 1½ hours. Remove the veal and keep warm.

3. Pour the contents of the roasting pan into a large saucepan and bring to a boil over high heat. Add the chipotles, zest, chile powder, honey, and salt and pepper to taste. Reduce the heat to medium and simmer for 20 minutes, skimming. Add the lemon juice. Process the sauce to a chunky consistency in a blender or food processor, or in the saucepan with a hand-held blender. *The meat and sauce may be made up to 1 day ahead and refrigerated together, covered.* Reheat, stirring, just before serving.

4. For each serving, place a piece of meat on a plate and spoon the sauce over it. Garnish with queso fresco. Serve immediately.

Makes 6 servings

Roasted Chicken
with Fresh Sage, Garlic, & Red Chile Oil

Aromatics give this dish its character. Chicken is roasted with sage, garlic, and chile-flavored oil, then these accents are incorporated into a spicy vinaigrette for saucing the bird. Each bite of chicken is hot, crisp, and juicy all at once.

2 chickens (2½ pounds each)
½ cup sage leaves
4 garlic cloves
½ cup Red Chile Oil
1 teaspoon Dijon mustard
2 teaspoons red wine vinegar
1 teaspoon minced red onion
2 cloves roasted garlic (page 8)
2 tablespoons ancho chile powder
Salt and freshly ground pepper

1. Preheat the oven to 500° F.

2. Stuff the chickens with the sage (reserving 5 leaves for the sauce) and garlic, truss the chickens, and brush generously with the chile oil. Roast for 45 minutes, remove from the oven, and keep warm. Degrease the pan drippings and set aside. You should have 1 cup.

3. In a blender, combine the mustard, vinegar, onion, reserved leaves of sage, roasted garlic, and chile powder. With the motor running, slowly add the drippings until emulsified. Season to taste with salt and pepper.

4. Let the chicken stand for 10 minutes before carving. Cut each chicken in half and serve with the sauce.

Makes 4 servings

Red Chile Oil

½ cup peanut oil
2 tablespoons ancho chile powder
1 jalapeño
3 cloves roasted garlic (page 8)
Salt and freshly ground black pepper

Combine the oil, chile powder, jalapeño, and garlic in a food processor and puree. Season to taste with salt and pepper. *May be made up to 2 days ahead.*

Makes ½ cup

Red Chile Duck

We cook this duck Asian style, but with Southwestern ingredients. Wrapped in a flour tortilla with crunchy Pineapple–Red Onion Relish (page 78), it makes a subtle but complex package of flavors.

3 Long Island ducklings (about
   4½ pounds each), skin pricked all
   over with a fork

MARINADE:
2 tablespoons ground white pepper
3 tablespoons ground cinnamon
3 tablespoons ground ginger
½ cup (packed) brown sugar
¼ cup red wine vinegar
2 tablespoons sesame oil
½ cup peanut oil
3 tablespoons ground fennel seed
1 tablespoon pureed canned chipotles
2 tablespoons ancho chile powder

12 flour tortillas
1 cup Pineapple–Red Onion Relish
   (page 78)

1. About 8 hours or 1 day before serving, prick the skin of the ducks all over with a fork. In a large pot over high heat, bring 8 quarts of water to a rapid boil and blanch the ducks for 5 minutes. Remove the ducks from the water and set aside.

2. In a medium saucepan, combine the marinade ingredients, bring to a boil, and remove from the heat immediately. Brush the ducks generously with the spice mixture and let marinate, refrigerated, for 4 to 6 hours or overnight.

3. About 2 hours before serving, preheat the oven to 350° F.

4. Roast the ducks, breast side up, for 1½ hours. Remove from the oven and let rest at room temperature for about 20 minutes.

5. In a dry skillet over medium-high heat, heat the flour tortillas for about 30 seconds. Carve the breast from each duck and slice very thin on the bias, allow-ing half a breast per person. Take a tortilla, spread a little relish on it, and place the sliced duck over that. Then wrap it up.
Makes 6 servings

5/97 Easy & Excellent

Roast Leg of Lamb
with Red Chile Crust

This lamb roasts in its marinade and when it is done, each slice is surrounded by a crisp, dark crust. Jalapeño Preserves (page 120) are perfect as a condiment. I once prepared this roast for a demonstration of how to cook several courses together in one oven. Along with the lamb, I made Sweet Potato Gratin with Smoked Chiles and a Peach and Blueberry Cobbler. It was a great meal—it was also a big oven.

3 tablespoons ancho chile powder
1 tablespoon pasilla chile powder
1 tablespoon toasted cumin
   seeds (page 9)
2 tablespoons olive oil
Salt and freshly ground black pepper
1 leg of lamb, boned and tied
   (about 6 pounds)

1. Combine the chile powders, cumin, oil, and salt and pepper to taste in a bowl. Rub the lamb on all sides with the marinade and allow it to rest at room temperature for about 2 hours.

2. Preheat the oven to 450° F.

3. Place the lamb in a roasting pan and roast for 15 minutes. Reduce the oven temperature to 350° F. and roast for 1 hour more, or until brown. Let the lamb rest at room temperature for 15 minutes before slicing. Serve immediately.
Makes 8 to 10 servings

Roast Leg of Lamb with Red Chile Crust, opposite

Smoked Pork Loin

with Apricot-Serrano Chile Sauce

Katy Sparks, my talented sous-chef, came up with this sauce one day when she was experimenting in the kitchen. Cold-smoking the pork infuses it with smoky flavor without cooking it. Then it is quickly grilled on the barbecue and served with this intensely flavored—though mild-looking—sauce. Serve this with Larry's Oregano Spoonbread (page 156).

**5 pounds boneless pork loin, cold-smoked
for 20 minutes (page 7)
1 recipe Apricot-Serrano Chile Sauce**

1. Prepare a wood or charcoal fire and let it burn down to embers, or preheat the broiler.

2. Slice the pork ½ inch thick, then pound the slices ¼ inch thick.

3. Grill the meat about one and a half minutes on each side, until the meat shows visible grill marks.

4. To serve, place 4 slices of pork loin on each individual plate and drizzle the sauce over it.

Makes 12 servings

Apricot-Serrano Chile Sauce

**½ cup dried apricots
2 serranos, roasted and peeled
1 tablespoon fresh lime juice
2 tablespoons red wine vinegar
¼ cup fresh orange juice
¼ cup olive oil
Salt and freshly ground pepper**

Combine all the ingredients in a blender and blend until emulsified. *Reserve the sauce for up to 2 days, refrigerated, in a squeeze bottle.*

Makes about 1 cup

Grilled Pork Chops Adobo

with Spicy Apple Chutney

Awesome

easy

This is the Southwestern version of a dish I grew up with, pork chops and applesauce. The pork chops are transformed by sitting overnight in an adobo marinade, and Spicy Apple Chutney is light-years beyond the applesauce on Mom's dinner table.

3 cups Adobo Marinade
8 loin pork chops 1 inch thick
3 cups Spicy Apple Chutney

1. The day before serving, pour the marinade over the pork chops, cover, and refrigerate overnight.

2. When you are ready to cook the pork, prepare a charcoal or wood fire and allow it to burn down to embers, or preheat the broiler.

3. Remove the chops from the marinade and reserve the marinade. Grill or broil the chops for 5 minutes on each side, brushing with marinade, until brown.

4. Remove the chops to a serving platter. Serve immediately, topped with chutney to taste. Serve extra chutney in a bowl in the center of the table.

Makes 4 servings

Adobo Marinade

2 cups drained canned tomatoes
3 tablespoons ancho chile powder
3 tablespoons pasilla chile powder
1 canned chipotle, seeded and diced
1 tablespoon honey
1 tablespoon dark brown sugar
3 tablespoons red wine vinegar
1 teaspoon cayenne
¼ cup chopped garlic
¼ cup olive oil

Puree the marinade ingredients in a food processor. *May be prepared up to 2 days ahead and refrigerated.*

Makes 3 cups

Spicy Apple Chutney

2 medium oranges
2 tablespoons unsalted butter
½ cup coarsely chopped red onion
1 tablespoon minced jalapeño
2 tablespoons finely diced ginger
2 cups fresh orange juice
½ cup red wine vinegar
½ cup (packed) light brown sugar
¼ cup honey
8 medium Granny Smith apples, peeled, cored, halved, and thinly sliced
2 tablespoons coarsely chopped cilantro
2 tablespoons finely diced red bell pepper
Salt and freshly ground pepper

1. Peel the oranges, reserving the zest, and cut the flesh into segments. Set aside.

2. In a large saucepan over medium heat, melt the butter and sauté the onion and jalapeño until the onion is translucent. Add the ginger, orange zest, orange juice, vinegar, brown sugar, and honey and cook until the sauce is reduced by half and has a glazed appearance.

3. Reduce the heat to low, add two-thirds of the apple spices, and cook until the fruit is just tender. Turn off the heat and gently fold in the remaining apples and the orange segments.

4. Pour the chutney into a bowl and allow to cool. Mix in the cilantro, red bell pepper, and salt and pepper to taste. *Pour into jars and refrigerate, covered, up to 3 days.* Bring to room temperature 1 hour before serving.

Makes 8 cups

Grilled Pork Chops Adobo with Spicy Apple chutney, opposite

Turragon *not great* *great*

Grilled Chicken Breasts
with Corn & Grilled Pepper Relish

Chicken breasts can be bland, but not with this fresh ginger and garlic marinade. The corn and pepper relish adds crunch and fresh vegetable flavor.

GINGER AND GARLIC MARINADE:
- 1 cup soy sauce, preferably low-sodium
- ½ cup coarsely chopped fresh ginger
- ½ cup coarsely chopped garlic
- ¼ cup fresh lime juice
- ¼ cup honey

- 6 skinless and boneless chicken breasts, halved
- 1 cup Corn and Grilled Pepper Relish

1. Combine all the marinade ingredients in a small saucepan and bring to a boil. Remove from the heat and refrigerate until cool.

2. Add the chicken breasts to the marinade and let marinate, refrigerated and covered, for 8 hours or overnight.

3. Prepare a wood or charcoal fire and let it burn down to embers, or preheat the broiler.

4. Remove the chicken breasts from the marinade and pat dry, discarding the marinade. Grill or broil the chicken for about 4 minutes on each side.

5. Serve immediately, with the relish spooned over.
Makes 6 servings

Corn & Grilled Pepper Relish

Balsamic vinegar gives this relish sweetness and great flavor, unlike other relishes that are made tart with lime juice.

- 1 cup roasted corn kernels (page 8)
- ½ cup finely diced roasted red bell pepper (page 8)
- 1 tablespoon finely diced red onion
- 1½ tablespoons balsamic vinegar
- 1½ tablespoons coarsely chopped cilantro
- ½ jalapeño, minced
- 1½ tablespoons olive oil
- **Salt and freshly ground pepper**

Combine the corn, pepper, onion, vinegar, cilantro, jalapeño, and oil in a bowl and season to taste with salt and pepper. *May be refrigerated, covered, for up to 1 day.*
Makes about 2½ cups

Venison
with Spicy Black Grape Sauce

Black grapes have an affinity for jalapeños as well as for venison, as this unusual sauce proves. The venison cooks in minutes, since it is extremely lean. Serve Horseradish Potatoes (page 145) or the Sweet Potato Gratin with Smoked Chiles (page 152)—both creamy with a surprising kick—to accompany the dish.

    4 venison medallions, from the loin
      or leg (6 ounces each)
    Salt and freshly ground pepper
    2 tablespoons olive oil
    1 cup Spicy Black Grape Sauce

1. Preheat the oven to 350° F. Season the venison medallions with salt and pepper.

2. In a large ovenproof sauté pan over medium-high heat, heat the oil and sauté the meat for 1 minute on each side. Place in the oven and roast for about 3 minutes. Let the venison rest at room temperature for 3 minutes.

3. Slice thin and serve with the grape sauce.

Makes 4 servings

Spicy Black Grape Sauce

Roasting the garlic for this sauce makes a big difference, and it's easy to do. See page 8 for directions.

    1 tablespoon unsalted butter
    2 tablespoons finely chopped red onion
    1 tablespoon finely chopped roasted
      garlic (about 3 cloves)
    1 teaspoon minced jalapeño
    ½ cup port
    ½ cup red wine
    1 cup Chicken Stock (page 16)
    ¼ cup undiluted grape juice concentrate
    ½ cup fresh or bottled grape juice
    ½ cup sliced seedless black grapes
    Salt and freshly ground white pepper

1. In a medium saucepan over medium-high heat, melt the butter and sweat the onion, garlic, and jalapeño for about 5 minutes. Raise the heat to high, add the port, and reduce 10 minutes to 1 tablespoonful. Add the red wine and reduce another 10 minutes to 1 tablespoonful. Add the stock and grape juice concentrate and reduce by two-thirds. Add the grape juice and reduce by half.

2. Strain the sauce through a fine sieve, return it to the saucepan, and reduce the heat to low. Add the grapes, cook for 5 minutes, and season to taste with salt and pepper. *May be made up to 2 days ahead and refrigerated, covered.* Reheat, stirring, just before serving.

Makes about 1 cup

Yucatán-style Chicken Skewers
with Papaya-Tomatillo Salsa

This is a good way to prepare chicken thighs or legs. The skewers make lively party hors d'oeuvres, with the salsa highlighting the sizzling chicken.

1 cup Yucatán Marinade (page 100)
9 skinless and boneless chicken thighs
1 medium jícama, julienned
Thirty-six 6-inch wooden skewers, soaked
**   in water for about 2 hours**
2 cups Papaya-Tomatillo Salsa

1. Rub the marinade into the chicken thighs. Cover the chicken and refrigerate for 4 to 6 hours or overnight.

2. Prepare a charcoal or wood fire and let it burn down to embers, or preheat the broiler.

3. Thread each piece of chicken onto 2 skewers so that the meat stays flat on the grill. Grill for about 4 minutes on each side, or until done to taste. For each serving, arrange 3 chicken thighs on a plate with the jícama and the salsa.
    Makes 6 servings

5/97 Used boneless skinless Whole Chicken breasts delish with Salsa

Papaya-Tomatillo Salsa

~~2~~ large papaya, peeled, seeded, and *(handwritten: X)*
**   coarsely chopped**
4 medium tomatillos, husked and coarsely chopped
~~2 tablespoons~~ finely diced red onion *(handwritten: 1 whole onion)*
1 tablespoon minced jalapeño
¼ cup fresh lime juice *(handwritten: 1/3 cup)*
¼ cup coarsely chopped cilantro *(handwritten: 1/2 C)*
1 teaspoon honey
Salt and freshly ground pepper

    Combine the papaya, tomatillos, onion, jalapeño, lime juice, cilantro, and honey in a bowl and season to taste with salt and pepper. *May be refrigerated for up to 1 day, covered.* Bring to room temperature before serving.
Makes about 3 cups

excellente

Barbecued Duck
with Yellow Corn Pancakes & Mango-Tomatillo Salsa

This is a visually appealing dish, with its yellows, dark reds, greens, and oranges—and each color brings its own flavor to the composition. I sometimes wrap this same duck and roasted corn filling in a soft flour tortilla and douse each taco in Smoked Red Pepper Sauce (page 64), one of my "mother sauces." In either case, the different elements can be prepared in advance and the dish assembled at the last minute.

  3 duck legs, skin removed
  1 cup New Mexico–style Barbecue Sauce
     (page 36)
  3 cups Chicken Stock (page 16)
  1 cup roasted corn kernels (page 8)
  3 tablespoons chopped cilantro
  Salt and freshly ground pepper
  4 Yellow Corn Pancakes
  1 cup Mango-Tomatillo Salsa

1. Preheat the oven to 300° F.

2. Brush the duck legs with barbecue sauce, place in a baking pan, and pour the stock around them. Cover the pan with aluminum foil, place in the oven, and cook for 3 hours, or until the duck is done. *May be prepared up to 2 days ahead and refrigerated.*

3. Shred the duck meat and discard the bones. In a sauté pan over medium heat, cook the duck meat, corn, and cilantro until heated through. Season to taste with salt and pepper. *May be cooked up to 2 days ahead and refrigerated.* Bring to room temperature before using.

4. Mound a fourth of the duck mixture in the center of each pancake and wrap the pancake around the filling. Place, seam side down, on a plate and garnish with 2 tablespoons of the salsa.

  Makes 4 servings

Yellow Corn Pancakes

½ cup yellow cornmeal
½ cup all-purpose flour
1 teaspoon baking powder
Salt
2 tablespoons honey
1 large egg, beaten
½ cup plus 2 tablespoons milk
1 tablespoon unsalted butter, melted

1. In a mixing bowl, combine the cornmeal, flour, baking powder, a pinch of salt, and honey. In a separate bowl, combine the egg, milk, and melted butter, add to the dry ingredients, and mix well. *May be prepared up to 1 day ahead, covered, and refrigerated.*

2. Heat a griddle or cast-iron frying pan over high heat and drop the batter by spoonfuls to make four 5-inch pancakes. Cook pancakes until brown on both sides and set aside, stacked and covered with foil.

Makes four 5-inch pancakes

Mango-Tomatillo Salsa

1 large mango, peeled, seeded, and coarsely
   chopped (page 7)
4 medium tomatillos, husked and coarsely chopped
2 tablespoons finely diced red onion
1 tablespoon minced jalapeño
¼ cup fresh lime juice
¼ cup coarsely chopped cilantro
1 teaspoon honey
Salt and freshly ground pepper

Combine the mango, tomatillos, onion, jalapeño, lime juice, cilantro, and honey in a bowl and season to taste with salt and pepper. *Refrigerate covered for up to 1 day.* Bring to room temperature before serving.

Makes about 3 cups

Chile-rubbed Guinea Hen

with Cranberry-Apricot Relish

When you sear the guinea hen, make sure the olive oil is very hot: The cornmeal coating should cook quickly, just enough to turn crisp and get a touch of brown color. Then put the hen in the oven so it can cook through. It will be spicy and crisp on the outside and juicy on the inside. Guinea hen legs may be substituted for duck legs in the Barbecued Duck and Wild Mushroom Quesadilla (page 36).

CURRIED CORNMEAL:
2 cups yellow cornmeal
1 tablespoon Curry Powder (page 6),
    or good-quality Madras curry powder
1½ teaspoons ground cumin
Salt and freshly ground pepper

4 boneless and skinless guinea hen breast
    halves or chicken breast halves
1 cup olive oil
¾ cup Cranberry-Apricot Relish

1. Combine the cornmeal, curry powder, cumin, and salt and pepper to taste and spread in a baking pan. Coat the hen breasts generously and evenly with the ancho puree, then dredge them in the seasoned cornmeal.

2. Preheat the oven to 400° F.

3. In a large ovenproof sauté pan over high heat, heat the oil until it begins to smoke and cook the breasts on 1 side for about 2 minutes, or until the topping is crisp. Turn the hens, cook on the other side until crisp, and put into the oven to cook for 5 minutes more, or until cooked through. Serve each breast topped with some relish.

Makes about 4 servings

Cranberry-Apricot Relish

This is a rowdy cranberry relish, not at all sedate like the one you remember from Thanksgivings past.

2 tablespoons unsalted butter
½ cup finely diced red onion
2 tablespoons finely julienned peeled ginger
2 jalapeños, minced
2 cups (1½ bags) cranberries, rinsed
    and picked over
2 cups fresh orange juice
2 tablespoons brown sugar
½ cup honey
¼ pound dried apricots, julienned
1 tablespoon Curry Powder (page 6) or good-
    quality Madras curry powder
Salt and freshly ground pepper

1. In a medium saucepan over medium heat, melt the butter and sweat the onion, ginger, jalapeños, and half the cranberries for 5 minutes, until the cranberries are wet.

2. Raise the heat to high, add the orange juice, brown sugar, and honey, and bring to a boil. Reduce the heat to medium and simmer for 10 minutes. Add the remaining cranberries and simmer for 5 minutes. Add the apricots, curry powder, and salt and pepper to taste. Mix well and remove from the heat. Pour the relish into a shallow pan to cool at room temperature. When cool, pour into a bowl and refrigerate. *May be refrigerated, covered, up to 3 days.*

Makes about 4 cups

vegetables

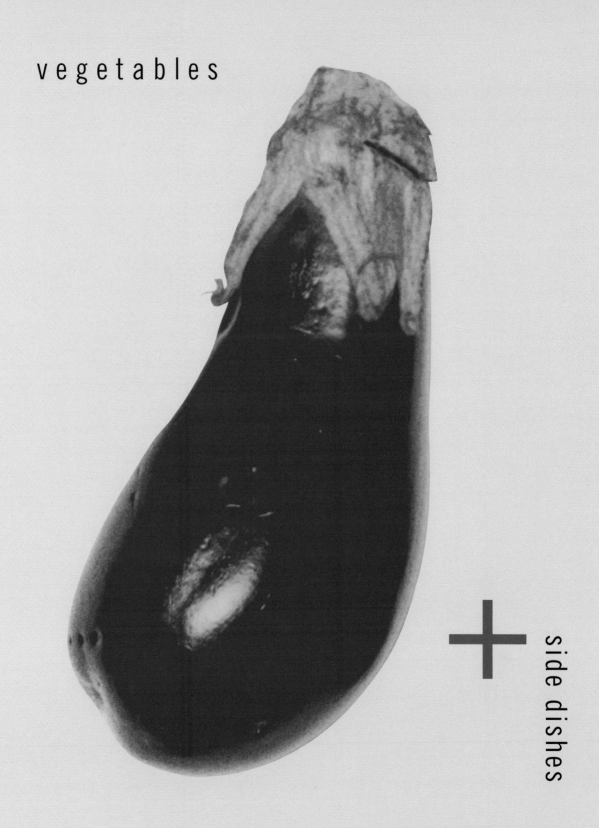

+ side dishes

you could feast on this abundant harvest of

greens, reds,

You could feast on this abundant harvest of vegetable dishes and nothing else, losing yourself happily in a forest of greens, reds, purples, and golds. From nut-sweet root vegetables to leafy greens, to ripe corn, eggplant, and zucchini, the vibrant flavors and electric colors can almost make you forget about all other foods. Yet all these dishes make excellent accompaniments to meat, fish, and poultry, as well.

My vegetable recipes range from simply grilled broccoli, zucchini, eggplant, and bell peppers to hard-core Southwestern Green Chile and Potato Hash, Cornmeal-coated Chiles Rellenos with Spicy Black Bean Sauce, and Southwestern Fries. In between you can find all sorts of dishes that will make imaginative use of the best your market has to offer.

Your basic guide to deciding which vegetables you want to serve should be the seasons—see what's best at a particular time. In the spring and summer I use corn and red and yellow tomatoes liberally, along with zucchini and eggplant. Roasted Corn with Chipotle Butter, Thyme-marinated Tomatoes, Zucchini Tacos, and Cornmeal-fried Eggplant with Tomatoes are all great summer dishes. In the fall, things get a little heartier with Sweet Potato Polenta and Sweet Potato Gratin with Smoked Chiles. And in the winter they are heartier still, with Creamed Kale, Ancho Chile Risotto Cakes, and Potato Tacos with Roasted Poblano Sauce. Creamy Chick-pea Polenta, crisp Buttermilk Onion Rings,

yourself happily in a forest of

purples, + golds

and savory tortas of black beans or goat cheese and oregano are on call any time of year.

Corn is my favorite vegetable, maybe my favorite food, and I like it best at the height of summer, simply roasted and brushed with chipotle butter. At other times of the year, tamales and polentas fill my kitchen with the irresistible aroma of sweet corn. Cornmeal spans the seasons and carries an underlying corn flavor that works perfectly in polentas with sweet potato or roasted garlic, and in a spoonbread with fresh oregano, similar to a cornbread soufflé. It also makes an incredible breading for eggplant, giving it a flavorful crunch. Look for blue cornmeal, which is organically grown and especially tasty.

I like to combine chiles and other ingredients with vegetables to extend the range of tastes. Some knock-

out combinations: Green Chile and Potato Hash, in which roasted poblanos and red peppers, potatoes, and onions are turned into a crisp pancake; Horseradish Potatoes, which hit the palate with a hidden jolt of freshly grated horseradish in a creamy gratin; Black Rice, which gets its jet black color and earthy flavor from simmering in a black bean stock seasoned with jalapeño and garlic.

It's fun to give a Southwestern twist to familiar dishes from other cuisines, like Italian eggplant and tomatoes, risotto, and polenta—a way to overturn everyone's expectations of a vegetable dish and create a new classic.

Cornmeal-coated Chiles Rellenos

with Spicy Black Bean Sauce

When you bite into this stuffed chile, you first savor the crisp cornmeal crust. The next layer is the poblano pepper, and inside that, the creamy goat cheese. And then there's the black bean sauce it's served on. With all those textures and flavors working together, you can't go wrong.

The poblano is the perfect chile for stuffing. It is big enough and it usually is mild, with a great pepper flavor. But individual poblanos can vary in their heat and once in a while someone is frightened away from this dish after encountering a blistering chile relleno.

DARK BEER BATTER:
¾ cup dark beer
1 large egg, lightly beaten
¼ cup milk
1¼ cups all-purpose flour
1 tablespoon melted butter
Salt and freshly ground pepper

4 tablespoons crumbled goat cheese
4 tablespoons grated Monterey Jack
4 poblano peppers, roasted, seeded, and peeled (page 8)
2 cups yellow cornmeal
3 cups peanut oil
2 cups Spicy Black Bean Sauce
Mixed greens
Cilantro sprigs

1. In a mixing bowl, combine the beer, eggs, milk, flour, and melted butter and mix well. Add salt and pepper to taste and set aside.

2. Mix together the cheeses and stuff the peppers with them. Batter lightly and dredge in cornmeal.

3. In a large frying pan over high heat, heat the oil to 375° F., or until a drop of batter sizzles. Fry the peppers, turning, until lightly browned, about 4 min-utes. Drain briefly on paper towels. Serve hot. *May be made the same day and refrigerated, covered. Reheat in a 350° F. oven just before serving.*

4. Spoon a layer of black bean sauce on a plate and place a chile on top of the sauce. Garnish with greens and cilantro.
   Makes 4 first-course servings

Spicy Black Bean Sauce

2 tablespoons oil
1 medium onion, coarsely chopped
2 garlic cloves, minced
1 jalapeño, minced
1 cup white wine
3 cups cooked or canned black beans, drained
3 cups Chicken Stock (page 16)
2 tablespoons toasted cumin seeds (page 9)
Salt and freshly ground pepper
1 medium tomato, coarsely chopped
2 tomatillos, husked and coarsely chopped

1. In a large saucepan over medium heat, heat the oil and sweat the onion, garlic, and jalapeño. Add the wine, raise the heat, and reduce until the liquid is almost completely evaporated. Add the beans and stock, reduce the heat, and simmer for 30 minutes. Add the cumin and salt and pepper to taste. Place in a food processor, and process to a smooth puree. *May be refrigerated, covered, for up to 2 days.*

2. Before serving, bring to room temperature and add the tomato and tomatillos.
   Makes about 3 cups

great — but use electric fryer

Cornmeal-fried Eggplant
with Tomatoes

At the height of the season, this dish glows with the colors of bright red tomatoes and green basil. A breading of crisp yellow cornmeal adds texture to the fried eggplant.

2 large ripe tomatoes, peeled and diced
¼ cup finely diced red onion
2 tablespoons fresh lime juice
1 tablespoon olive oil
¼ cup basil chiffonnade
Salt and freshly ground pepper
4 baby eggplants or 1 medium eggplant
Olive oil
LIGHT BEER BATTER:
¼ cup all-purpose flour
1 large egg, lightly beaten
½ cup beer
2 tablespoons melted butter

¼ cup all-purpose flour
1 cup finely ground yellow cornmeal
4 cups peanut oil

1. In a mixing bowl, combine the tomatoes, onion, lime juice, olive oil, and basil. Season to taste with salt and pepper and set aside.

2. Preheat the oven to 400° F.

3. Slice the eggplant ¼ inch thick to make 16 slices. (You may have to cut large slices in half.) Season to taste with salt and pepper, toss lightly with olive oil, and arrange on a baking sheet in a single layer. Roast for 10 minutes or until tender but not too soft.

4. In a mixing bowl, combine the flour, egg, beer, melted butter, and salt and pepper to taste to make the batter. In another bowl, combine ½ cup flour with salt and pepper to taste. In a third bowl, combine the cornmeal with 1 tablespoon each salt and pepper.

5. Lightly dredge the eggplant slices in the flour, dip in the batter, shaking off the excess, and dredge in the cornmeal.

6. In a large saucepan over medium-high heat, heat the oil to 375° F., or until a drop of batter sizzles. Fry the eggplant, turning, for about 2 minutes on each side, or until golden. Remove and drain on paper towels.

7. To serve, lay 1 slice of eggplant on a plate, mound 2 tablespoons of tomatoes over it, and top with a second slice of eggplant. Serve immediately.
Makes 8 side-dish servings

Thyme-marinated Tomatoes

Beautiful red tomatoes perfumed with thyme are perfect piled on top of a grilled steak.

3 medium tomatoes, cut into ¼-inch
   dice (about 1 pound)
2 tablespoons minced fresh thyme leaves
1 rounded teaspoon finely chopped garlic
1 teaspoon olive oil
2 teaspoons red wine vinegar
Salt and freshly ground pepper

Combine the tomatoes, thyme, garlic, oil, and vinegar and mix well. Season to taste with salt and pepper. *May be refrigerated, covered, for up to 1 day.* Bring to room temperature before serving.
Makes 6 servings

Creamed Kale

Like creamed spinach, but heartier and more flavorful, creamed kale dresses up a winter meal.

- 2 pounds kale, center stalks removed
- 4 tablespoons unsalted butter
- 1 cup heavy cream
- ⅛ teaspoon ground nutmeg
- Salt and freshly ground pepper

1. Blanch the kale in lightly salted water until tender, rinse in ice water, and cut into ½-inch ribbons. *May be blanched up to 4 hours ahead and refrigerated.*

2. In a large sauté pan over medium heat, melt the butter and add the kale, cream, and nutmeg. Reduce the heat to low and cook for 5 minutes, or until the cream has reduced and thickened. Season to taste with salt and pepper.

Makes 6 to 8 servings

Horseradish Potatoes

Here is an elegant but hearty side dish for game or meats.

- 6 large potatoes, peeled and sliced crosswise ⅛ inch thick
- Salt and freshly ground pepper
- 1½ cups freshly grated horseradish
- 4 cups heavy cream

1. Preheat the oven to 400° F.

2. Make a layer of potato slices in a 12 x 12-inch casserole, season to taste with salt and pepper, and cover with ¼ cup of the horseradish. Coat with heavy cream. Repeat to yield 6 layers of potatoes, ending with potatoes.

3. Bake, uncovered, for 15 minutes, or until the top begins to brown. Cover with foil and bake for another 30 minutes, or until the potatoes are tender. *May be prepared up to 1 day ahead, covered, and refrigerated.* To serve, heat for 12 minutes in a 350° F. oven.

Makes 8 servings

Corn & Wild Rice Pancakes

These crunchy pancakes are a great side dish with poultry or fish.

2 large eggs, lightly beaten
2 tablespoons melted butter
2 cups whole milk
1½ cups all-purpose flour
1 teaspoon honey
½ teaspoon baking powder
¼ teaspoon canned pureed chipotles
1 cup cooked wild rice
6 scallions, chopped
¼ cup finely chopped cilantro
1 cup roasted corn kernels (page 8)
Salt and freshly ground pepper

1. In a mixing bowl, combine the eggs, melted butter, milk, flour, honey, and baking powder to make a batter. Add the pureed chipotles, wild rice, scallions, cilantro, corn, and salt and pepper to taste and mix well. *May be made up to 4 hours ahead and refrigerated.*

2. In a nonstick skillet over low heat, pour the batter in ¼- cup portions to form pancakes. Cook until brown, about 3 minutes, turn, and brown the other side. Serve immediately.

Makes 10 to 12 pancakes

Corn & Wild Rice Pancakes, opposite

made batter to recipe too watery add ½ cup more flour 1 Tablespoon Chipotes puree

Green Chile & Potato Hash

Colorful and lively, this dish complements any fish preparation. Served side by side with poached eggs, it is an eye-opener for brunch.

10 medium russet potatoes, peeled
   and cut into ¼-inch dice
5 tablespoons unsalted butter
3 tablespoons chopped red onion
1½ tablespoons chopped garlic
8 poblanos, roasted, peeled, seeded, and
   coarsely chopped (page 8)
2 red bell peppers, roasted,
   peeled, seeded, and coarsely chopped
   (page 8)
Salt and freshly ground pepper

1. In a large saucepan over high heat bring the potatoes and enough salted water to cover to a boil. Cook the potatoes until tender, about 30 minutes. Drain and set aside.

2. In a small skillet over low heat, melt 2 tablespoons of the butter and sweat the onion and garlic for 3 minutes. Add to the potatoes. Add the poblanos and bell peppers, and gently mix with a rubber spatula or wooden spoon. Season to taste with salt and pepper. *May be prepared up to 1 day ahead, covered, and refrigerated.*

3. In a large skillet over medium heat, heat the remaining butter. When it foams, form individual pancakes, using 1 cup of potato mixture each. Cook until golden brown on 1 side, about 3 minutes, turn, and brown the other side. Serve immediately.

Makes 12 cakes

Twice-baked Potatoes with Smoked Chiles

These savory stuffed potatoes are perfect with steak. The chiles add a surprising dimension of flavor.

 6 medium russet potatoes, scrubbed,
  dried, and individually wrapped in foil
 ½ pound soft goat cheese
 ½ cup thinly sliced scallions
 2 tablespoons pureed canned chipotles
 2 tablespoons unsalted butter
 ½ cup whole or low-fat milk
 Salt and freshly ground white pepper

1. Preheat the oven to 350° F.

2. Bake the potatoes for 1 hour, or until done, remove the foil, and let the potatoes cool at room temperature.

3. When they are cool enough to handle, cut off both ends and hollow out the potatoes, leaving the shells whole. Reserve the shells. Mash the potato flesh with the goat cheese, scallions, and chipotle puree.

4. In a small saucepan over medium heat, melt the butter with the milk, then beat it into the potato-cheese mixture and season to taste with salt and pepper. Stuff the reserved shells with the potato mixture. *May be prepared ahead up to this point on the same day, covered, and reserved at room temperature or refrigerated.* If refrigerated, bring to room temperature before reheating.

5. When ready to serve, preheat the oven to 400° F. Place the stuffed potatoes on a baking sheet and bake for 5 minutes, or until hot.

 Makes 6 servings

Zucchini Tacos

Tacos are good vehicles for fresh vegetables. Layered with crisp zucchini and chile-flavored cheese (or with potatoes and spicy green poblano sauce, as in the next recipe), they let you add new dimensions to familiar foods. Serve as a side dish with fish or poultry or as a first course with a salsa or relish of your choice.

 3 large zucchini, sliced lengthwise
  into thin ribbons
 Eight 6-inch flour tortillas, or 8-inch
  tortillas cut to size
 2 cups grated Texas caciotta cheese, or
  Monterey Jack with jalapeños
 Salt and freshly ground pepper
 Olive oil

1. Preheat the oven to 400° F.

2. For each serving, lay 4 slices of zucchini over half of a tortilla, sprinkle ¼ cup of the cheese over the zucchini, and season to taste with salt and pepper. Fold the tortilla over the filling to make a semi-circle. *May be prepared several hours ahead, covered, and refrigerated.* Before serving, brush lightly with olive oil, and bake until crisp and brown, about 6 minutes. Cut in half before serving.

 Makes 8 servings

Buttermilk Onion Rings

Serve these crisp, tangy rings with grilled shrimp. Sweet Vidalia or Spanish onions work best, but regular onions can be substituted.

1 cup all-purpose flour
3 cups buttermilk
Cayenne
Salt
6 large Spanish or Vidalia onions
4 cups peanut oil
2 cups seasoned flour (page 6)

1. Peel the onions, cut them crosswise into ¾-inch slices, and separate them into rings.

2. In a mixing bowl, combine the flour, buttermilk, and cayenne and salt to taste to make a batter. Soak the onion rings in the batter for 2 hours or longer in the refrigerator.

3. When ready to fry, heat the oil to 375° F., or until a drop of batter sizzles. Dredge the onion rings in seasoned flour and fry, turning, in batches, until tender and golden brown, 3 to 4 minutes. Drain on paper towels and season with salt. Serve immediately.

Makes 8 servings

Wild Rice
with Grilled Vegetables

The nutty flavor of wild rice contrasts with the sweet grilled vegetables in this dish. It goes well with poultry dishes.

2 tablespoons unsalted butter
1 large red onion, finely diced
1 tablespoon minced garlic
4 cups wild rice
1 head broccoli
1 medium red bell pepper, seeded and cut in half
1 medium yellow bell pepper, seeded and cut in half
1 medium zucchini, cut on the bias ½ inch thick
1 medium yellow squash, cut on the bias ½ inch thick
1 medium eggplant, cut on the bias ½ inch thick
Olive oil
Salt and freshly ground pepper

1. Prepare a wood or charcoal fire and let it burn down to embers, or preheat the broiler.

2. In a large saucepan over medium heat, melt the butter and sauté the onion and garlic for 5 minutes. Add the rice, stir, and add 3 quarts of water. Bring to a boil, then reduce the heat to medium and cook for 45 minutes, or until the rice is puffed and tender. Drain and set aside.

3. Meanwhile, blanch the broccoli in lightly salted water until tender, rinse in ice water, and break it into florets. Set aside.

4. Toss the broccoli, peppers, zucchini, yellow squash, and eggplant in the olive oil, season to taste with salt and pepper, and grill or broil until tender, about 3 minutes on each side.

5. Cut the zucchini, yellow squash, and eggplant into ¼-inch matchsticks about 2 to 3 inches long and coarsely chop the bell peppers. Add the vegetables to

the cooked rice and season to taste with salt and pepper. To reheat, melt 1 tablespoon butter in a saucepan over medium heat and add the rice. Cook until hot.

Makes 8 to 10 servings

Roasted New Potatoes
with Cilantro Pesto

For this beautiful dish, simply toss roasted new potatoes over heat with pesto. Put this in the center of a table spread with tempting platters for a grand feast.

12 new potatoes, unpeeled
½ cup Cilantro Pesto (page 77)

1. Cut the potatoes into quarters and roast as described on page 8. *May be roasted 1 day ahead and refrigerated.*

2. In a large saucepan over medium heat, warm the potatoes, add the pesto, and mix until the pesto is evenly distributed over the potatoes. Serve warm.

Makes 4 servings

Cilantro Risotto Cakes

Start with delicate, herb-flavored risotto and turn it into fried cakes that are brown and crisp on the outside and creamy on the inside.

    4½ cups Chicken or Fish Stock (page16)
    Salt and freshly ground pepper
    6 tablespoons unsalted butter
    1½ tablespoons finely chopped
        red onion
    1 teaspoon finely chopped garlic
    1 pound Arborio rice
    ½ cup white wine
    2 cups chopped cilantro

1. In a large saucepan over high heat, combine the stock with enough salt to give it a slightly salty taste and bring to a boil. Set aside and keep warm.

2. In a large saucepan over low heat, melt 2 tablespoons of the butter and sweat the onion and garlic for 4 minutes. Add the rice, raise the heat to medium, and stir to coat the rice with butter. Cook, stirring, for 2 minutes. Add the wine and reduce by half, stirring constantly. Stir in 2 cups of the stock and cook, stirring frequently. When the liquid is almost completely absorbed, add 1 cup of stock and cook, stirring, until almost completely absorbed. Add the remaining stock and cook, stirring, until the risotto is very thick and the rice is al dente.

3. Remove from the heat, add the cilantro, and mix thoroughly. On a lightly oiled baking sheet, spread the rice in a 1-inch layer and *refrigerate, covered with plastic wrap, for at least 2 hours or up to 1 day ahead.*

4. When ready to serve, cut the risotto into 3-inch circles. In a large skillet over medium-high heat, melt the remaining butter and sauté the cakes until golden brown on both sides.
    Makes 10 to 12 cakes

Southwestern Fries

These shoestring fries sharply seasoned with ancho and cumin are great with steaks, fish, or just about anything else.

    ½ cup ancho chile powder
    2 tablespoons ground cumin
    2 tablespoons salt
    4 cups peanut oil
    4 large potatoes, sliced lengthwise into
        very thin shoestring strips

1. Combine the chile powder, cumin, and salt and set aside.

2. In a large saucepan over high heat, heat the peanut oil to 375° F., or until a bit of potato sizzles when immersed. Fry the potatoes in batches for about 3 minutes, or until crisp and golden brown. Drain on paper towels.

3. Immediately season with the spice mixture and serve.
    Makes 8 servings

Ancho Chile Risotto Cakes

Everyone loves risotto, but it can be hard to serve at a dinner party because it requires last-minute cooking and constant attention. This dish solves the problem. The risotto can be prepared ahead and refrigerated, then cut into circles and fried. These little cakes are wonderful with roasted lobster or grilled fish.

    2 tablespoons unsalted butter
    1 medium onion, chopped
    1 tablespoon chopped garlic
    1 pound Arborio rice
    2 tablespoons ancho chile powder
    5 cups Lobster Stock, heated (page 17)
    Salt and freshly ground pepper
    3 tablespoons minced fresh thyme leaves
    ½ cup peanut oil

1. In a large saucepan over medium heat, melt the butter and sweat the onion and garlic for 5 minutes. Add the rice and chile powder, stir, and sweat for 3 minutes more. Raise the heat to high, add 1 cup of the stock, and bring to a boil, stirring constantly. When the stock has been absorbed, continue to add hot stock 1 cup at a time, until all of it has been absorbed and the rice is cooked al dente. Season to taste with salt and pepper and stir in the thyme.

2. On a lightly oiled baking sheet, spread the rice in a 1-inch layer and *refrigerate, covered with plastic wrap, for at least 2 hours or up to 1 day ahead.*

3. When ready to serve, cut the risotto into 3-inch circles. In a large skillet over medium-high heat, heat the peanut oil to 375° F., or until a bit of risotto sizzles when immersed. Fry the cakes for 2 minutes on each side, or until brown. Serve as a side dish.
    Makes 10 to 12 cakes

Sweet Potato Gratin with Smoked Chiles

This dish is close to aphrodisiacal. As it bakes, the heavy cream is absorbed by the potatoes, so the gratin is firm, not creamy or soupy. The chipotle pepper adds a surprising jolt of spice.

    4 cups heavy cream
    1 canned chipotle pepper
    6 medium sweet potatoes, peeled
      and sliced thin
    Salt and freshly ground pepper

1. Preheat the oven to 350° F.

2. In a blender, puree the cream and chipotle until smooth.

3. In a 10 x 10-inch casserole, arrange a fourth of the sweet potatoes, season to taste with salt and pepper, and pour a fourth of the cream over all. Repeat with the remaining potatoes and cream, forming 4 layers. *May be prepared up to this point one half-hour ahead, covered, and refrigerated.*

4. Bake for 1 hour, or until the cream has been absorbed and the potatoes are browned. *May be prepared up to 1 day ahead, covered, and refrigerated.* To serve, reheat in a 350° F. oven for 12 minutes.
    Makes 8 to 10 servings

Opposite: Sweet Potato Gratin with Smoked Chiles, left, Horseradish Potatoes, right

Black Rice

Kevin Rathbun introduced me to this dish, which he prepared at the Baby Routh restaurant in Dallas, and it inspired me to try my own version. The idea is to use the black cooking liquid from black beans to cook rice. Use the beans for another dish, such as Black Bean–Goat Cheese Tortas (page 158), or Black Bean–Corn Salsa (page 84). Serve black rice with Red Snapper Roasted in Banana Leaves with Red Curry Sauce (page 97).

> 4 cups water or Chicken Stock (page 16)
> 1 pound dried black turtle beans
> 1 tablespoon unsalted butter
> ½ cup finely diced red onion
> 1 tablespoon minced garlic
> 2 cups long-grain white rice
> Salt and freshly ground pepper
> ¼ cup finely chopped cilantro

1. In a large saucepan over high heat, bring the water to a boil and add the beans, using just enough liquid to keep them covered. Cook until tender, 45 to 60 minutes, and drain, reserving the cooking liquid. Reserve the beans for another dish.

2. In a large saucepan over medium heat, heat the butter and sauté the onion and garlic until soft. Add the rice and stir to coat with butter. Add 4 cups of the reserved bean liquid (add water if necessary) and bring to a boil. Cover, reduce the heat to low, and simmer for 20 minutes. Season to taste with salt and pepper and stir in the cilantro. Serve immediately.

Makes 6 servings

Sweet Potato Polenta

In this very versatile dish, sweet potatoes add great flavor to polenta—you might say they wake up the cornmeal. Serve with softshell crabs, or any quail or chicken dish.

> 2½ pounds sweet potatoes, peeled and cut into medium cubes
> 1¾ cups finely ground yellow cornmeal
> ½ cup honey
> Salt and freshly ground pepper
> 3 tablespoons butter

1. In a large saucepan over high heat, cook the sweet potatoes in salted boiling water until tender, about 30 minutes. Drain, reserving 1 cup of the cooking water.

2. In a food processor, process the potatoes and as much of the reserved cooking liquid as needed into a puree. *May be made up to 1 day ahead, covered, and refrigerated.*

3. In a medium saucepan over high heat, bring to a rolling boil 4 cups of the puree and 4 cups of water. Add the cornmeal in a steady stream, whisking constantly. (Do not add it all at once, or the polenta will be lumpy.) As soon as all the cornmeal has been incorporated, reduce the heat to low and cook for 20 to 25 minutes, stirring occasionally. When the polenta pulls away from the sides of the pot as it is stirred, it is done. Add the honey, season to taste with salt and pepper, and pour into an 8 x 10-inch baking dish and refrigerate. *May be prepared 2 days ahead up to this point.*

4. When ready to serve, cut the polenta into 2-inch squares. In a large skillet over medium heat, melt the butter and sauté the squares until golden brown on both sides. Serve immediately as a side dish.

Makes 8 to 10 servings

Roasted Corn & Garlic Polenta

More savory than the sweet potato polenta, this is just as versatile. Try it with grilled shrimp or fish.

14 cloves roasted garlic, peeled (page 8)
4 cups finely ground yellow cornmeal
2 cups roasted corn kernels (page 8)
2 teaspoons freshly ground white pepper
3 tablespoons butter

1. In a blender or food processor, combine the roasted garlic with ½ cup water and process until pureed. Add a little more water, if necessary.

2. In a medium saucepan over high heat, bring to a rolling boil 10 cups of water, 1 tablespoon salt, and the pureed garlic. Add the cornmeal in a steady stream, whisking constantly. (Do not add it all at once, or the polenta will be lumpy.) As soon as all the cornmeal has been incorporated, reduce the heat to low and cook for 20 to 25 minutes, stirring occasionally. When the polenta pulls away from the sides of the pot as it is stirred, it is ready. Add the corn and cook for 5 minutes more. Stir in the pepper and salt to taste. Pour the polenta into an 8 x 10-inch baking dish and refrigerate. *May be prepared 2 days ahead up to this point.*

3. When ready to serve, cut the polenta into 2-inch squares. In a large skillet over medium heat, melt the butter and sauté the squares until golden brown on both sides. Serve immediately as a side dish.
Makes 8 to 10 servings

Chick-pea Polenta

This is a hearty accompaniment to pork chops.

2 cups cooked or canned chick-peas, drained
1 cup finely ground yellow cornmeal
1 tablespoon ground cumin
Salt and freshly ground pepper
3 tablespoons butter

1. In a food processor, process the chick-peas to a coarse consistency. Set aside.

2. In a large saucepan over high heat, bring to a rolling boil 3 cups water and add the cornmeal in a steady stream, whisking constantly. (Do not add it all at once, or the polenta will be lumpy.) As soon as all the cornmeal has been incorporated, reduce the heat to low and cook for 20 to 25 minutes, stirring occasionally. When the polenta pulls away from the sides of the pot as it is stirred, it is ready. Add the chick-pea puree and the cumin and cook for 5 minutes longer. Season to taste with salt and pepper. Pour into an 8 x 10-inch baking dish and refrigerate. *May be prepared 2 days ahead up to this point.*

4. When ready to serve, cut the polenta into 2-inch squares. In a large skillet over medium heat, melt the butter and sauté the polenta squares until golden brown on both sides. Serve immediately as a side dish.
Makes 8 to 10 servings

Roasted Corn
with Chipotle Butter

Instead of serving roasted corn with plain butter, we infuse the butter with chipotles for a surprising, smoky flavor.

8 ears roasted corn (page 8)
¼ cup Chipotle Butter (page 125)

Before serving, preheat the broiler and reheat the corn, turning until evenly heated. Brush with the compound butter and serve.
Makes 8 servings

Larry's Oregano
Spoonbread

This has always been one of my simplest recipes, but when my cook Larry Manheim prepared it for a party we gave in Philadelphia at Jack's Firehouse restaurant, it took him three hours, for a host of reasons. When we got there at nine in the morning, Jack McDavid, the gregarious owner, immediately offered Larry some moonshine whiskey. He followed that with a dried habañero chile that blew Larry's mouth away. Ingredients like roasted garlic, grated cheese, and chives can be hard to find in someone else's kitchen, and the moonshine was making Larry dizzier by the minute. Anything that could have gone wrong that morning did. This uncomplicated spoonbread gave Larry the hardest time of his life, so my spoonbread is his now—he's famous for it.

3 cups whole milk
1½ cups finely ground yellow cornmeal
6 large eggs, separated
6 cloves roasted garlic, peeled and roughly chopped (page 8)
1½ cups buttermilk
3 tablespoons unsalted butter, melted
2 teaspoons baking powder
¾ teaspoon baking soda
1½ teaspoons salt
1 tablespoon sugar
Cayenne
⅔ cup grated parmesan
½ cup finely chopped fresh oregano
½ cup finely chopped chives

1. Preheat the oven to 350° F.

2. In a small saucepan over high heat, bring the milk to a boil, and remove from the heat. Set aside.

3. Pour the cornmeal into a large mixing bowl and add the hot milk, stirring. Add the egg yolks, garlic, buttermilk, butter, baking powder, baking soda, salt, sugar, and cayenne to taste. Combine well.

4. Beat the egg whites until stiff. Fold the whites and ⅓ cup of the parmesan into the batter. Fold in the oregano and chives.

5. Butter a 12 x 12-inch casserole and sprinkle with half the remaining cheese. Pour in the batter and sprinkle with the remaining cheese. Bake for 40 to 45 minutes, or until the top is golden and the spoonbread is soft. Cut into squares and serve hot.
Makes 10 to 12 servings

vegetables & side dishes

Potato Tacos
with Roasted
Poblano Sauce

Serve potato tacos as a side dish with steak.

    12 new potatoes
    ¼ cup olive oil
    Salt and freshly ground pepper
    Six 6-inch flour tortillas, or 8-inch
        tortillas cut to size
    1½ cups grated Texas caciotta cheese
        or Monterey Jack with jalapeños
    2 tablespoons ancho chile powder
    ½ cup Roasted Poblano Sauce
        (page 64)

1. Preheat the oven to 400° F.

2. Rub the potatoes with half of the oil and season them to taste with salt and pepper. Place them on a baking sheet and roast for 40 minutes, or until done. Cut the potatoes into ¼-inch-thick slices.

3. Using 1 tortilla for each serving, place ½ cup of cheese over half the tortilla's surface, top with 2 sliced new potatoes, and season to taste with salt and pepper. Fold the tortilla over the filling to make a semicircle. *May be prepared to this point up to 1 day ahead, covered, and refrigerated.* Before serving, brush the top lightly with oil, and sprinkle with ancho chile powder. Bake for 6 minutes, or until crisp. Cut each taco in half and drizzle with sauce.

Makes 6 servings

great & easy

Goat Cheese &
Oregano Tortas

Make sure you use fresh oregano in these tortas; then serve them as an accompaniment to rabbit or other game, or any poultry.

    20 flour tortillas about 3 inches in
        diameter, cut from larger tortillas
    1 cup crumbled goat cheese
    1 cup grated Monterey Jack
    ½ cup finely diced red onion
    2 tablespoons chopped fresh
        oregano leaves
    Salt and freshly ground pepper
    Olive oil

1. Preheat the oven to 500° F.

2. For each torta, arrange 5 tortillas on a work surface. Combine the cheeses, onion, and oregano and season to taste with salt and pepper. Spread the mixture evenly over 4 of the tortillas. Stack the tortillas, with the plain tortilla on top, and press down lightly so the layers stick together. Brush the top with olive oil and bake for 5 minutes, until the tortas are crisp on top and the cheese has melted inside.

Makes 4 servings

Black Bean–Goat Cheese Tortas

You need to get flavor into black beans because alone they are boring, so season them well. Goat cheese can be dry, but the white cheddar will help it melt and will make the tortas moist—sort of a buddy system of cheeses. Serve this with any poultry dish.

2 cups cooked or canned
 black beans, drained
2 tablespoons ground cumin
Salt and freshly ground pepper
20 flour tortillas about 3 inches in
 diameter, cut from larger tortillas
1½ cups grated goat cheese
1 cup grated white cheddar
Olive oil
1 tablespoon ancho chile powder

1. Preheat the oven to 500° F.

2. In a food processor, puree the beans with the cumin and salt and pepper to taste until smooth.

3. For each torta, arrange 5 tortillas on a work surface. Spread the black bean puree thinly and evenly on 4 of the tortillas and sprinkle with the cheeses and salt and pepper to taste. Stack the tortillas with the plain tortilla on top, and press down lightly so the layers stick together. Brush the top with olive oil and sprinkle with ancho powder. Bake for 5 minutes, until the tortas are crisp on top and the cheese has melted inside. *May be assembled and refrigerated several hours before baking.*

 Makes 4 servings

Black Bean–Goat Cheese Torta, above

breads

+ sandwiches

+ chips

with breads like these to build on, you won't want to make ...

ordinary

sandwiches

t he hearty breads I bake complement the assertive foods I serve, although they are substantial enough to be served alone. They are standing by to sort of put out the fire, to absorb the heat of chiles and curries.

These breads are corn inspired. The chewy rolls get their texture from the yellow cornmeal that is mixed into the dough and sprinkled on top before baking. Both blue cornbread and yellow cornbread carry the flavor and the crunch of cornmeal. Most of these breads are fairly quiet because they are meant to be served with spicy dishes. But sometimes a bread comes with its own fireworks, and then the foods that accompany it have to be a little calmer. Chipotle Brioche is a buttery loaf that holds waves of chipotle flavor. The bread adds a wonderful chile piquance to sandwiches, but the rule here is: Don't use anything too spicy in a sandwich when the heat is in the bread.

With breads like these to build on, you won't want to make ordinary sandwiches. The brioche is the foundation for my Swordfish Club Sandwich, which has a terrific range of colors and flavors. A cornmeal roll provides a more neutral base for slices of grilled pork loin flavored by adobo, then dressed with a Sage Aioli. I also use the roll for a Smoked Shrimp Sandwich with Basil-Garlic Dressing, and for a soft-shell crab sandwich with Ancho Mayonnaise.

Combinations like these are a little more complicated than peanut butter and jelly, and they deserve to be the center of attention. Build a lunch, brunch, or even an informal supper around them. Put out bowls of Ancho Chile Potato Chips or Southwestern Fries (page 151), pour some cold beer or margaritas, and follow the sandwiches with more sandwiches— Fudge Brownie Cookie and Banana Swirl Ice-Cream Sandwiches (page 190).

Spicy chips are good to munch on as a snack or with drinks, but they can also provide imaginative vehicles for many other foods. Try Avocado Relish (page 38) generously heaped on Blue Corn Chips, or caviar and crème fraîche on Ancho Chile Potato Chips. Plantain Croutons go well with Spicy Salmon Tartar (page 92), and Blue Corn Flatbread is perfect with paper-thin slices of Tequila-cured Salmon (page 87). Simple as these dishes are, they will add your signature to the table.

Chipotle Brioche

Stephan Pyles, author of *The New Texas Cuisine*, first introduced me to this bread and inspired this recipe. Don't attempt it without a strong electric mixer.

1 envelope active dry yeast
2 tablespoons sugar
1¼ cups warm whole milk
8 cups all-purpose flour
1½ tablespoons salt
2 large eggs
7 large egg yolks
¼ cup pureed canned chipotles
¾ pound (3 sticks) unsalted butter, plus
   a little for rubbing the tops of the loaves, at room
   temperature

1. In a small bowl, combine the yeast, sugar, and milk. Allow to sit until foamy, about 10 minutes.

2. In a mixer bowl, combine the flour and salt. Mixing with a dough hook on low speed, add the yeast mixture. Gradually add the eggs, egg yolks, pureed chipotles, and the butter and continue mixing for 15 minutes, until silky and springy.

3. Leave the dough in the mixer bowl, cover, and set the dough in a warm place to rise for 1 hour, or until doubled. Punch down, cover with plastic wrap, and allow to rise for 30 minutes more. Shape the dough into 2 loaves, being careful to press out any air, and place in 12 x 4 x 4-inch loaf pans. Rub the tops with butter and allow to rise for 2 hours, covered with plastic wrap, in a warm place.

4. Preheat the oven to 350° F.

5. Bake 25 minutes or until firm on top. (When you press it, your finger shouldn't go through the crust.) Cool in the pans.
   Makes 2 loaves

Assorted breads, left

Mesa Grill Dinner Rolls

These rolls are the creation of Mesa Grill's pastry chef, Wayne Brachman. They have a sweet corn flavor and are robust enough to accompany spicy foods. They are best made with an electric mixer. Bake them double size to use for the Blue Corn–Softshell Crab Sandwich (page 174).

½ cup warm water
1 tablespoon sugar
1 envelope active dry yeast
1 tablespoon salt
¾ cup coarsely ground
    yellow cornmeal
1 cup whole milk
2 tablespoons dark brown sugar
5¼ to 6 cups all-purpose flour
Egg wash, made from 1 large egg
    lightly beaten with 1 teaspoon water
Coarse cornmeal, for sprinkling
    on the rolls

1. Preheat the oven to 350° F.

2. In a small bowl, combine the water, sugar, and yeast and set aside in a warm place until bubbling, about 10 minutes.

3. In a large saucepan over high heat, bring 1 cup water to a boil with the salt. Add ½ cup of the cornmeal, whisking constantly until the mixture returns to a boil. Remove from the heat immediately and set aside.

4. Combine the milk, brown sugar, cooked cornmeal, the yeast mixture, and 5¼ cups flour in the bowl of an electric mixer equipped with a dough hook and turn the machine to its lowest setting. Mix for 15 minutes, adding more flour if the dough sticks to the bowl. The dough should be smooth, elastic, and slightly sticky. Cover with a damp towel and put in a warm place to rise for 10 to 15 minutes, until it increases in volume by about one-third.

5. Line a baking pan with lightly buttered parchment paper. Roll the dough into a thick rectangle. For each dinner roll, shape a ball of dough about the size of a small lime and place on the pan. Cover with plastic wrap and let rise in a warm place until almost double in volume, about 25 minutes. Score the top of each roll once with a sharp knife, brush with egg wash, and sprinkle with cornmeal. Bake for 7 minutes, then turn the pan a quarter turn and bake 7 minutes more, until they sound hollow when tapped on the bottom. Cool in the pan.
Makes 12 rolls

breads, sandwiches & chips

Blue Cornbread

I always find the sweet flavor of blue cornmeal appealing. Blue carries even more corn flavor than yellow cornmeal, perhaps because the corn is organically grown and milled in small quantities.

½ pound (2 sticks) unsalted butter,
    at room temperature
2 cups coarsely ground blue cornmeal
2 cups all-purpose flour
2 tablespoons baking powder
2 large eggs, lightly beaten
2 teaspoons salt
2⅔ cups buttermilk

1. Preheat the oven to 400° F.

2. In a food processor, combine the butter, cornmeal, flour, baking powder, eggs, and salt. Process 20 to 30 seconds, until just mixed. You may have to do this in 2 batches. Pour in the buttermilk and process for 20 seconds more. Pour into a buttered 12 x 12-inch pan, and bake for 40 to 45 minutes, until firm to the touch and golden. Cut into 3-inch squares.

Makes 16 pieces

Chipotle Cornbread

The smokiness of chipotles heightens the taste of corn. Try the bread spread generously with Jalapeño Preserves (page 120) for brunch or a snack.

1 cup coarsely ground yellow cornmeal
1 cup all-purpose flour
2 tablespoons sugar
1 teaspoon salt
1½ teaspoons baking powder
1 large egg, lightly beaten
½ cup buttermilk
½ cup milk
6 tablespoons unsalted butter, melted
4 canned chipotles, pureed
Shortening

1. Preheat the oven to 450° F. and preheat two 6-inch cast-iron skillets in the oven for 20 minutes.

2. In a mixing bowl, combine the cornmeal, flour, sugar, salt, and baking powder. Fold in the egg, buttermilk, milk, butter, and pureed chipotles.

3. Brush the preheated pans with shortening and immediately pour in the batter, approximately three-fourths of the way up. Bake for 25 minutes, or until the cornbread is brown around the edges and firm. Cut each cornbread into 4 wedges.

Makes 8 pieces

breads, sandwiches & chips

Blue Corn Flatbread

Bake this bread very thin to ensure a crisp texture. Serve with Tequila-cured Salmon (page 87).

½ cup coarsely ground blue cornmeal
½ cup all-purpose flour
½ teaspoon salt
¾ cup water

1. Preheat the oven to 350° F.

2. Combine the cornmeal, flour, and salt in the bowl of an electric mixer fitted with a paddle beater. Stir in the water and mix for 5 minutes, or until smooth.

3. Pour the mixture onto a 12½ x 17-inch baking sheet lined with buttered parchment paper and spread very thin with a spatula.

4. Bake for 10 minutes, give the sheet a quarter turn, and bake for 4 more minutes, or until crisp. To serve, break into portions by hand.

Makes 12 servings

Swordfish Club Sandwich on Chipotle Brioche

This elegant sandwich is composed of brightly colored layers of fish, greens, tomato, and avocado on orange brioche.

2 tablespoons peanut oil (optional)
4 swordfish steaks (about 5 ounces each)
Salt and freshly ground pepper
12 slices Chipotle Brioche, ¼ inch thick, toasted (page 165)
⅓ cup Avocado Vinaigrette (page 73)
Mesclun or young lettuce
4 slices ripe tomato
1 Haas avocado, peeled, halved, and thinly sliced

1. If grilling the swordfish, prepare a wood or charcoal fire and let it burn down to embers. If broiling, preheat the broiler. If sautéing, heat the oil in a large sauté pan over medium heat.

2. Season the fish on both sides with salt and pepper to taste and cook until medium, by your method of choice.

3. For each sandwich, lay 3 slices of brioche side by side. Spread 2 slices with vinaigrette. Place a small handful of mesclun on 1 slice of brioche and top with a slice of tomato. On the next slice, place the fish and a fourth of the avocado slices. Stack the 2 slices and top with the third. Cut the sandwich in half on the diagonal.

Makes 4 sandwiches

Smoked Shrimp Sandwich

with Basil-Garlic Dressing

Fresh basil, crisp greens, and smoked shrimp make a great summer sandwich. It is best served at room temperature.

28 medium shrimp (about 1 pound)
½ cup olive oil
1 celery stalk, thinly sliced
4 cups mesclun or mixed young
  lettuce leaves
½ cup thinly sliced scallions
½ cup Basil-Garlic Dressing
Salt and freshly ground pepper
4 Mesa Grill Dinner Rolls, cut in half
  and toasted (page 166)
4 slices ripe tomato
¼ cup basil chiffonnade

1. Cold-smoke the shrimp for 15 to 20 minutes as described on page 7.

2. In a large skillet over medium-high heat, heat the olive oil and sauté the shrimp until cooked through, 2 to 3 minutes.

3. In a large bowl, toss the shrimp, celery, mesclun, and scallions with the dressing until evenly coated. Season to taste with salt and pepper.

4. For each sandwich, mound the shrimp salad on half a roll, allowing 7 shrimp per sandwich. Top with the tomato, basil, and the remaining half roll.

Makes 4 sandwiches

Basil-Garlic Dressing

2 tablespoons diced red onion
1 teaspoon minced garlic
1 tablespoon Dijon mustard
1 tablespoon good-quality mayonnaise
4 tablespoons fresh lime juice
¾ cup olive oil
½ cup (firmly packed) basil leaves
Salt and freshly ground pepper

In a blender, combine the onion, garlic, mustard, mayonnaise, and lime juice and blend until pureed. With the motor running, slowly add the olive oil until emulsified. Add the basil leaves and blend until smooth. Season to taste with salt and pepper. *May be prepared up to 1 day ahead, covered, and refrigerated.*

Makes 1 cup

Pork Adobo Sandwich
with Sage Aioli

This hearty sandwich has become a lunchtime staple at Mesa Grill. For the filling, marinate thin slices of pork tenderloin in the same sweet and spicy marinade that you use for pork chops and grill them very quickly. The pork is cooled by the herbal aioli.

1½ pounds pork tenderloin
1½ cups Adobo Marinade (page 131)
Salt and freshly ground pepper
¼ cup Sage Aioli
1 large tomato, cut into 8 slices
8 lettuce leaves
4 Mesa Grill Dinner Rolls (page 166), or
  other 4-inch rolls
3 cups Ancho Chile Potato Chips
  (page 173)

1. Cut the meat into ½-inch-thick slices and pound very thin. You should have 16 slices. Pour the marinade over the pork slices and marinate for 1 hour, refrigerated.

2. Prepare a wood or charcoal fire and let it burn down to embers, or preheat the broiler. Season the pork with salt and pepper to taste and grill for 2 minutes on each side. Set aside.

3. For each sandwich, layer 4 slices of pork, 1 tablespoon aioli, 2 slices tomato, and 2 lettuce leaves between halves of a roll. Garnish with chips.

Makes 4 sandwiches

Sage Aioli

½ cup good-quality mayonnaise
1½ teaspoons minced garlic
1 tablespoon fresh sage chiffonnade
1 tablespoon fresh lemon juice

Combine the mayonnaise, garlic, sage, and lemon juice in a bowl. *May be prepared up to 2 days ahead of time, covered, and refrigerated.* Bring to room temperature before serving.

Makes ½ cup

Blue Corn Chips

These chips and the Ancho Chile Potato Chips are great for parties. I like to set out bowls of different colored salsas with the chips as a tempting centerpiece.

4 cups peanut oil
Twenty 6-inch blue corn tortillas,
cut into quarters
Salt

In a large saucepan or deep fryer, heat the oil to 375° F., or until a piece of tortilla sizzles when immersed. Fry the chips a few at a time until crisp, about 2 minutes. Drain on paper towels and season to taste with salt. *May be prepared up to 2 days ahead and stored covered.*
Makes 80 chips

Plantain Croutons

I serve these slightly banana-flavored croutons with Spicy Salmon Tartar (page 92), and they add great crunch to salads.

2 green plantains
2 cups peanut oil
Salt

1. Peel the plantains and slice them paper thin lengthwise, using a mandoline.

2. In a large saucepan over high heat, heat the peanut oil to 375° F., or until a slice of plantain sizzles when it is immersed. Fry the plantain slices for 3 minutes, or until crisp. Drain on paper towels and season with salt to taste while still hot. *These may be made 2 days ahead and stored covered.*
Makes 6 servings

Ancho Chile Potato Chips

Homemade potato chips are always the best, and these sing with the spicy, fruity flavor of ancho chile powder.

4 cups peanut oil
8 large potatoes, peeled and
sliced as thin as possible
½ cup ancho chile powder
Salt

In a large saucepan or deep fryer, heat the oil to 375° F., or until a piece of potato sizzles when immersed. Fry the chips a few at a time until crisp and golden, about 2 minutes. Drain on paper towels and, while still wet, toss with the chile powder and salt to taste. *These may be made 2 days ahead and stored covered.*
Makes 8 cups

breads, sandwiches & chips

Blue Corn–Softshell Crab Sandwich

The crisp blue cornmeal coating contrasts nicely with the delicate softshell crab. Make sure you don't over-cook the crab.

½ cup all-purpose flour
½ cup coarsely ground blue cornmeal
2 large eggs, lightly beaten
4 softshell crabs, cleaned
Salt and freshly ground pepper
2 tablespoons oil
1 tablespoon butter
Lettuce
Tomato slices
4 double-size Mesa Grill Dinner Rolls
   (page 166)
¼ cup Ancho Mayonnaise

1. Place the flour, cornmeal, and eggs in separate bowls and season each to taste with salt and pepper.

2. Dredge each crab in flour, shake off the excess, and dip into the eggs, covering completely. Dredge in cornmeal.

3. In a medium skillet over medium heat, heat the oil. Add the butter and when it begins to foam, cook the crabs 2 to 3 minutes on each side, or until crisp.

4. For each serving, place 1 crab on half a roll and cover with lettuce and tomato slices to taste. Top with the mayonnaise and the remaining half roll.
   Makes 4 sandwiches

Ancho Mayonnaise

1 cup good-quality mayonnaise
3 tablespoons Ancho Puree (page 8)
4½ teaspoons fresh lime juice
4½ teaspoons chopped cilantro
Salt and freshly ground pepper (optional)

Combine all the ingredients in a mixing bowl and whisk until smooth. *May be prepared up to 2 days ahead, covered, and refrigerated.* Bring to room temperature before serving.
Makes about 1¼ cups

desserts

are baked into

cobblers,

crisps

+ pies.

these fruit desserts are light, not overly sweet,

and c a l m i n g to a palate that has just had an

electrifying adventure

with  +

chiles   garlic

the desserts that I most like to prepare—and eat—are simple. Emphasizing big flavors and distinctive textures rather than technique, they are truly American. My favorites are filled with fragrant, juicy fruits and berries and topped with buttery pastry or crisp sweetly spiced crumbs. Fresh berries, peaches, apples, and mangoes are baked into cobblers, crisps, and pies. These fruit desserts are light, not overly sweet, and calming to a palate that has just had an electrifying adventure with chiles and garlic.

Pumpkin Bread Pudding is a soothing yet robust creation, dense and warm. A silky Vanilla Bean Flan is dressed with an utterly simple sauce of berries whisked in a blender with a little sugar and lemon. In Wild Rice Pudding with Caramel Sauce, extra texture and flavor are added to an old standby.

With desserts, I don't topple idols so much as I embellish them. If you like the original tarte tatin, with apples baked in a bubbling caramel sauce under a flaky crust, try my Southwestern version made with mangoes. With Maple Sugar–Crusted Apple Pie, by slightly changing something very familiar, you call it to new heights. Chocolate Polenta Soufflé Cakes combine light cornbread with a chocolate soufflé (one that cannot fall), and add as a bonus a center of the richest melted chocolate imaginable. And banana ice-cream sandwiches on fudge brownies are your old friends from the ice-cream wagon, given new energy.

delish great put lots of pekans too

Peach & Blueberry Cobbler

delish great put lots of pekans too

desserts

A simple dessert and my favorite. Use the freshest with and ripest fruit and you will be rewarded with a sweet, juicy cobbler with a beautiful purple-blue color and the intoxicating aromas of summer. Toast the pecans before you mix them into the topping to keep them crisp.

    12 ripe peaches, peeled and
        sliced into eighths
    2 cups blueberries, roughly chopped
    3½ tablespoons sugar
    1 tablespoon fresh lemon juice
TOPPING
    1 cup all-purpose flour
    ½ cup sugar
    2 teaspoons baking powder
    1 cup heavy cream
    1 tablespoon cider vinegar
    ½ teaspoon salt
    3 tablespoons butter
    3 tablespoons shortening
    1 cup chopped, toasted pecans (page 9)

1. Preheat the oven to 400° F.

2. In a mixing bowl, toss the peaches, blueberries, sugar, and lemon juice.

3. To prepare the topping, in the bowl of an electric mixer, combine the flour and sugar. Add the cream, vinegar, a pinch of salt, butter, baking powder, and shortening and mix well. Mix half the pecans into the topping.

4. Pour the fruit into an 8 x 12 x 2-inch baking dish, spread the topping on top, and sprinkle with the remaining pecans. Bake for 30 minutes, or until the topping is browned and cooked through. Serve warm.

Makes 6 servings

Apple-Blackberry Crisp with Cinnamon Ice Cream

This crisp was a milestone for me—it was one of the first desserts I did that worked perfectly. The ice cream complements both the blackberries and the topping.

    2 cups all-purpose flour
    1 teaspoon ground nutmeg
    1 teaspoon ground ginger
    ½ cup (packed) light brown sugar
    8 tablespoons (1 stick) unsalted butter,
        cold, cut into pea-size pieces
APPLE-BLACKBERRY FILLING
    10 medium Granny Smith apples, peeled, cored,
        quartered, and the quarters cut into thirds
    ½ cup (packed) light brown sugar
    2 teaspoons ground cinnamon
    ½ teaspoon ground nutmeg
    ½ teaspoon ground ginger
    2 cups blackberries
    1 quart Cinnamon Ice Cream (recipe opposite)

1. To prepare the topping, combine the flour, nutmeg, ginger, and brown sugar in the bowl of an electric mixer and turn the machine to its lowest setting. Add the butter gradually and mix to a coarse meal. Scoop up handfuls of the mixture and rub it between your palms to form large crumbs. Refrigerate ½ hour or overnight.

2. Preheat the oven to 375° F.

3. To prepare the filling, in a mixing bowl, toss the apple with the brown sugar, cinnamon, nutmeg, and ginger. Gently fold in the blackberries.

4. Lightly butter a 12 x 12-inch baking dish and spoon in the fruit filling. Sprinkle a thick, even layer of crumb topping over the filling. Cover and bake for 10 minutes. Uncover and bake for 25 minutes more. Serve warm with ice cream.

Makes 8 servings

Cinnamon Ice Cream

2 cups whole milk
2 cups heavy cream
1 teaspoon ground cinnamon
1 large cinnamon stick
1 cup sugar
9 large egg yolks

1. In a small saucepan over medium heat, combine the milk, the cream, the ground and stick cinnamon, and 1 tablespoon of the sugar and scald.

2. Whisk the yolks and the remaining sugar together to blend. While whisking, slowly drizzle the hot milk mixture into the eggs to warm them. Pour this mixture into the saucepan of milk and cook over low heat for about 10 minutes, stirring constantly with a wooden spoon. When the custard begins to thicken enough to coat the spoon, strain and chill.

4. Freeze in an ice-cream maker according to manufacturer's directions. Remove to a bowl, cover and wrap in plastic, and store in the freezer up to 2 weeks.

Makes 2 quarts

Apple–Blackberry Crisp with Cinnamon Ice Cream, right

Mango Tarte Tatin

desserts

This play on the classic tarte tatin made with apples requires care in preparing the fruit. Mangoes melt a lot faster than apples do, so watch them carefully when you cook them with the sugar.

1½ cups all-purpose flour
1 tablespoon sugar
6 tablespoons unsalted butter, cold, cut into pea-size bits
1 large egg, lightly beaten with 1 cup water
MANGO FILLING:
3 firm but ripe mangoes
1 cup sugar
6 tablespoons unsalted butter

1. To prepare the pastry, combine the flour and sugar in the bowl of an electric mixer and turn the motor to the lowest speed. Add the butter and mix until the consistency of coarse meal. Drizzle in just enough egg mixture to hold the dough together and discard the rest. Cover the dough with plastic wrap and refrigerate for at least 2 hours.

2. Roll out the chilled dough to a 9-inch round, wrap in plastic, and refrigerate while preparing the mangoes.

3. Preheat the oven to 350° F.

4. To prepare the filling, peel the mangoes and cut into 1-inch slices.

5. In a 9-inch ovenproof skillet over medium-high heat, melt the butter and sugar and cook to a very light caramel syrup, about 5 minutes. Arrange the mango slices over the syrup in a pinwheel pattern and cook for 5 minutes, or until the caramel turns medium brown.

6. Place the skillet in the oven and bake for 10 minutes. Cover the mango slices with the dough and bake for 15 to 20 minutes, or until the crust is golden brown. Remove from the oven, let the tart rest for 2 minutes, then invert it onto a serving platter. *It may be made 1 day ahead, sliced into wedges, and refrigerated, covered.*

Makes 8 servings

Raspberry Cup Custard with Graham Cracker Crust

Fresh raspberries lighten a creamy, rum-flavored custard in this cool dessert.

1 cup graham cracker crumbs
½ cup plus 2 tablespoons sugar
5 tablespoons unsalted butter, melted
2 cups heavy cream
6 large egg yolks
1 tablespoon vanilla extract
1 tablespoon dark rum
36 fresh raspberries
Sugar for glazing (optional)

1. Preheat the oven to 300° F. and set a rack in the middle.

2. In a small mixing bowl, combine the graham cracker crumbs, ½ cup of the sugar, and the melted butter. Divide the mixture among six ⅔-cup custard cups and press down to form a crust on the bottom.

3. In a small saucepan over medium heat, combine the cream and 1 tablespoon of the remaining sugar. Scald and remove from the heat. In a large mixing bowl, combine the yolks, the remaining tablespoon of sugar, vanilla, and rum. Whisk lightly, just to combine.

4. Whisking lightly, gradually drizzle the scalded cream mixture into the egg mixture to warm it without scrambling the eggs. Strain the mixture and pour into the custard cups. Place 6 raspberries in each cup, dunking them so they are coated with custard.

5. Arrange the cups in a roasting pan and pour in hot water halfway up the sides. Cover the pan with foil and bake for 30 to 40 minutes, or until the custards are set. Cool in the pan, then *refrigerate, covered, up to 2 days ahead.*

6. If you like, sprinkle a light layer of sugar over each custard and place under a preheated broiler for about 2 to 4 minutes, watching that they don't burn. Serve immediately after glazing.

Makes 6 servings

Vanilla Bean Flan
with Fresh Berry Sauce

Here is another dessert that contrasts a rich custard with juicy fresh berries. Nothing interrupts the berries' intense, summery taste.

2 cups sugar
VANILLA BEAN CUSTARD:
  3 cups whole milk
  1 cup cream
  1 vanilla bean, split, scraped,
    and the seeds reserved
  6 large eggs
  8 large egg yolks
  1 tablespoon vanilla extract

1½ cups Fresh Berry Sauce

1. Preheat the oven to 300° F. and set a rack in the middle.

2. To prepare the syrup, in a heavy saucepan, combine 1 cup of the sugar with ¼ cup water. Bring to a boil over high heat and boil until amber colored and syrupy, about 5 minutes. Divide the syrup among eight ⅔-cup custard cups, swirling to coat the cups halfway up. Set aside.

3. To prepare the custard, in a small saucepan over medium heat, combine the milk, cream, 2 tablespoons of the remaining sugar, and the vanilla seeds and scald. Remove from heat.

4. In a large mixing bowl, combine the eggs, yolks, vanilla, and the remaining sugar. Whisking lightly, gradually drizzle the scalded cream mixture into the egg mixture to warm it without scrambling the eggs. Strain the mixture and pour into the custard cups.

5. Arrange the cups in a roasting pan and pour in hot water halfway up the sides. Cover the pan with foil and bake for 30 to 40 minutes, until the custards are set. Cool in the pan. *May be done to this point up to 2 days ahead and refrigerated, covered.*

6. To serve, run a knife around the edge of each custard and invert onto a plate. Serve with berry sauce.

Makes 8 servings

Fresh Berry Sauce

2 cups strawberries, raspberries, or
  blackberries, or any combination
½ cup sugar
1 tablespoon fresh lemon juice

  In a food processor, combine all the ingredients and process for 2 to 3 minutes. Strain out any seeds. *May be prepared up to 2 days ahead and refrigerated, covered.*

Makes 1½ cups

Maple Sugar– crusted Apple Pie

The flavors of maple sugar, maple syrup, and apples combine in this most American of desserts. Serve it with homemade Vanilla Ice Cream.

2 cups all-purpose flour
¼ cup plus 2 tablespoons maple sugar
½ teaspoon salt
12 tablespoons (1½ sticks) unsalted butter, cut into pea-size bits and frozen
2 tablespoons shortening, cut into pea-size bits and frozen
¼ cup ice water, mixed with a few drops of lemon juice
APPLE FILLING:
10 to 12 medium Granny Smith or McIntosh apples, peeled, cored, quartered, and then cut into thirds (10 cups)
¼ cup sugar
2 teaspoons ground cinnamon
1 teaspoon ground nutmeg
¼ cup cornstarch
2 tablespoons arrowroot
¼ cup maple syrup
1 large egg, lightly beaten with 2 tablespoons water

1. To prepare the pie dough, combine the flour, 2 tablespoons of the maple sugar, and salt into the bowl of an electric mixer and turn the machine to its lowest setting. Add the frozen butter gradually and mix for 5 minutes, or until the butter starts to break up. Add the frozen shortening and mix for 2 to 3 minutes more. Drizzle in the ice water, just enough for the dough to start to mass together. Let the dough rest for 10 minutes, form into 2 discs, and refrigerate for 30 minutes. *May be made 3 days ahead and refrigerated, covered.*

2. Preheat the oven to 400° F.

3. To prepare the filling, in a mixing bowl, combine the apples, sugar, cinnamon, nutmeg, cornstarch, and arrowroot. Add the maple syrup and mix gently.

4. On a floured surface, roll out 1 circle of dough and place in a 10-inch pie pan. Add the apple filling. Roll out the second crust, lay it over the filling, and crimp the edges. Brush the top crust with the egg wash, sprinkle with half the remaining maple sugar, and cut several vents in the crust.

5. Bake the pie for 30 minutes. Reduce the oven temperature to 350° F., sprinkle the remaining sugar over the top crust, and bake for 30 minutes more, or until the apple filling is bubbling. Should be baked and served the same day.
    Makes 6 to 8 servings

Vanilla Ice Cream

1 vanilla bean
1 tablespoon vanilla extract
2 cups whole milk
2 cups heavy cream
1 cup sugar
9 large egg yolks

1. Split the vanilla bean and scrape out the seeds. Place the bean and its seeds, the vanilla extract, milk, cream, and 1 tablespoon of the sugar in a small saucepan over medium heat and scald.

2. Whisk the yolks and the remaining sugar together to blend. While whisking, slowly drizzle the hot milk mixture into the eggs to warm them. Then pour this mixture into the saucepan of milk and cook over low heat, stirring constantly with a wooden spoon, for about 10 minutes. When the custard begins to thicken enough to coat the spoon, strain and chill.

4. Freeze in an ice-cream maker according to manufacturer's directions. Remove to a bowl, cover and wrap in plastic, and store in the freezer for up to 2 weeks.
    Makes 2 quarts

Pumpkin Bread Pudding

Instead of the usual pumpkin pie after a Thanksgiving feast, try this fragrant pudding, rich with autumn colors and spices.

PUMPKIN BREAD:
- 1¾ cups sifted all-purpose flour
- ¼ teaspoon baking powder
- 1 teaspoon baking soda
- 1 teaspoon salt
- 1 teaspoon ground cinnamon
- ½ teaspoon ground cloves
- ¾ cup sugar
- ⅓ cup shortening
- 2 large eggs
- 1 cup canned pumpkin puree
- ⅓ cup milk
- 1 teaspoon vanilla extract
- ½ cup coarsely chopped pecans

PUMPKIN CUSTARD:
- 1 cup whole milk
- 1 cup cream
- ½ cup sugar
- 5 large egg yolks
- ¼ cup canned pumpkin puree
- 1 teaspoon vanilla extract
- ¼ teaspoon ground cinnamon
- ¼ teaspoon ground nutmeg
- ¼ teaspoon ground ginger

1. At least one day before preparing the pudding, make the pumpkin bread.

2. Preheat the oven to 350° F.

3. Sift together the flour, baking powder, baking soda, salt, cinnamon, and cloves.

4. In a separate bowl, beat together the sugar, shortening, and eggs until fluffy. Add the pumpkin, milk, and vanilla and mix well. Add the dry ingredients and pecans to the pumpkin mixture and mix well. Pour into an oiled 9 x 5 x 2½-inch loaf pan and bake for 1 hour, or until firm and brown. *May be baked up to 4 days early or frozen 2 weeks.* When the bread is cool enough to handle, slice half of it ¾ inch thick and break the slices into chunks about 1-inch square. Leave out uncovered overnight to get stale. Reserve. (Serve the remaining half as a breakfast bread.)

5. When you are ready to prepare the pudding, preheat the oven to 300° F.

6. In a medium saucepan over medium-high heat, scald the milk, cream, and 2 tablespoons of the sugar.

7. Place the egg yolks, pumpkin, vanilla extract, cinnamon, nutmeg, ginger, and remaining sugar in a mixing bowl and whisk together. Slowly drizzle in the hot milk, whisking to combine the ingredients, then add the bread cubes and mix. Pour into a buttered 2-quart pan, place in a larger pan, and pour hot water half way up the sides. Bake for 50 minutes, or until set. *May be prepared several hours ahead and reserved at room temperature (don't reheat).*

Makes 6 servings

Pumpkin Bread Pudding, opposite

Wild Rice Pudding
with Caramel Sauce

A rice pudding can be bland, but not this one made with wild rice. It is gilded with caramel.

- ½ cup wild rice
- 8 cups whole milk
- 1 vanilla bean, split, scraped, and seeds reserved
- 1½ cups sugar
- 1 cup converted white rice
- 1 large egg
- 2 large egg yolks
- 2 teaspoons vanilla extract
- 1 tablespoon ground cinnamon
- 2 teaspoons ground nutmeg
- 2 cups Caramel Sauce (recipe follows)

1. In a medium saucepan over high heat, bring 4 cups of water to a boil. Add the wild rice, reduce the heat to medium, and simmer until the rice is tender, about 40 minutes. Drain and reserve.

2. In a large saucepan over high heat, bring the milk to a boil with the vanilla seeds and the sugar. Add the white rice. Reduce the heat to medium, cover, and simmer for 1 hour, or until tender and creamy. Add the wild rice and cook for 10 minutes more.

3. In a mixing bowl, lightly whisk the egg, egg yolks, and vanilla extract until blended. Whisk in a little of the hot rice to warm the mixture, then pour the egg mixture into the remaining hot rice. Cook, stirring, over low heat for 3 minutes. *Cool and refrigerate, covered, up to 1 day ahead.*

4. To serve, combine the cinnamon and nutmeg. Divide the pudding among 8 to 10 dessert bowls and sprinkle with the spices. Top with caramel sauce.

Makes 8 to 10 servings

Caramel Sauce

½ cup sugar
2 cups heavy cream

In a medium saucepan over low heat, combine the sugar and 2 tablespoons water and cook for 10 minutes, or until the sugar turns golden. Drizzle in the cream, mixing well. *May be prepared up to 2 days ahead, covered, and refrigerated.*

Makes about 2 cups

Pecan & White Chocolate Tart

desserts

This dessert is amazingly simple to prepare, but you must be careful about a few points. Paint the pastry with egg wash before you fill it to prevent leaks; if the filling leaks under the pastry shell during baking, you will have a hard time separating the dessert from its tin. Be sure to cover every pecan with syrup, or the nuts will burn. Finally, Myers's rum is my choice for this tart because it is aged in oak and has a high molasses content, giving it a deep, sweet flavor.

CRUST:
- 2 cups all-purpose flour
- 2 tablespoons sugar
- 12 tablespoons (1½ sticks) unsalted butter, cut into ½-inch dice
- 3 tablespoons ice water
- 1 large egg, lightly beaten

PECAN FILLING:
- 1 cup sugar
- 5 large eggs, lightly beaten
- 1 cup plus 2 tablespoons dark corn syrup
- 6 tablespoons unsalted butter, melted
- 2 tablespoons dark rum, preferably Myers's
- 1 tablespoon vanilla extract
- 2½ cups pecan halves or pieces

3 ounces white chocolate

1. To prepare the pastry, in the bowl of an electric mixer, combine the flour, sugar, and butter and mix, preferably with the paddle attachment, until the consistency of coarse meal. Add ice water to form a soft dough. Pat the dough into a disc, cover with plastic wrap, and refrigerate 2 hours or until firm.

2. Preheat the oven to 400° F.

3. Roll out the dough into a 14-inch circle and place it in an 11-inch tart pan with a removable bottom. Line the shell with foil, weight it down with dried beans, and bake for 20 minutes. Remove the beans and foil and bake for 3 minutes more. Brush the shell with the beaten egg and bake for 3 minutes more. Set aside the baked pastry shell. Reduce the oven heat to 325° F.

3. To prepare the filling, in a mixing bowl, combine the sugar, eggs, corn syrup, butter, rum, and vanilla extract. Whisk just to blend. Arrange the pecans in the baked pastry shell and pour the sugar mixture over them, making sure that every nut is covered. Bake, uncovered, for 30 to 35 minutes, or until brown and firm. Let cool at room temperature.

4. Melt the chocolate in a double boiler over very low heat, stirring with a wooden spoon until completely melted. Use a fork to drizzle the warm chocolate vigorously over the finished tart. *May be prepared up to 2 days ahead and refrigerated, covered.* Before serving, remove the sides of the pan and slice the tart.

Makes 12 servings

Fudge Brownie Cookie & Banana Swirl Ice-Cream Sandwiches

I flatten chewy brownies into rich cookies and spread a generous layer of homemade banana ice cream between two of them for my version of the venerable ice-cream sandwich. It is more luxurious, chocolaty, and fragrant than anything you might remember from long ago.

You may want to double the recipe and freeze the second batch, well covered in plastic wrap, to serve at another time.

BANANA ICE CREAM:
    1 cup heavy cream
    1 cup milk
    4 large egg yolks
    ½ cup sugar
    1½ very ripe bananas
BROWNIE COOKIES:
    3 ounces semisweet chocolate
    1 cup all-purpose flour
    ¾ teaspoon baking powder
    ¼ teaspoon salt
    8 tablespoons (1 stick) unsalted butter
    ½ cup sugar
    1 large egg, lightly beaten
    1 teaspoon vanilla extract
    ¾ cup chopped toasted walnuts
       or pecans (page 9)

1. To make the ice cream, in a heavy saucepan over medium heat, combine the milk and cream. Scald and set aside.

2. In a mixing bowl, beat the eggs with ⅓ cup of the sugar. Gradually whisk in the cream mixture. Return the mixture to the saucepan and cook, stirring constantly, over low heat, for about 7 minutes, or until thickened. Do not let it come to a boil.

3. Pour the mixture back into the bowl and place in a larger bowl filled with ice. Cool for 1 hour, stirring occasionally.

4. In a food processor, puree the bananas with the remaining sugar. Fold into the chilled cream mixture and freeze in an ice-cream maker according to manufacturer's directions. *May be prepared ahead, covered, and reserved in the freezer up to 2 weeks.*

5. To prepare the fudge brownie cookies, preheat the oven to 375° F. and grease a cookie sheet.

6. In the top of a double boiler over medium-high heat, melt the chocolate. Let cool at room temperature. Mix together the flour, baking powder, and salt and set aside.

7. In the bowl of an electric mixer, cream the butter and sugar. Mix in the egg, then stir in the melted chocolate, flour, and vanilla. Fold in the nuts.

8. Drop rounded tablespoons of the batter onto the cookie sheet and flatten to form 2½-inch round cookies. Bake 7 to 8 minutes, until cooked but still soft. *May be prepared ahead and refrigerated on the cookie sheet.*

9. To assemble each sandwich, allow the ice cream to soften slightly, spread 1 cookie thickly with ice cream, and top with a second cookie. Wrap in plastic and reserve in the freezer until ready to serve, or up to 1 week.
    Makes 6 servings

desserts

Candied Lime Tart

You don't have to be a pastry chef to prepare this impressive tart, but the custard, though simple, can trip you up. Once it starts to boil, don't leave it for a second. Keep on whisking, or it will scramble and you will have to start again.

1½ cups all-purpose flour
4 teaspoons sugar
½ teaspoon salt
10 teaspoons unsalted butter, cut into
  pea-size pieces
1 large egg, lightly beaten with ½ cup water
CANDIED LIME:
1 cup sugar
Zest of 2 limes, cut into 2 x ⅛-inch strips
LIME CUSTARD:
1 tablespoon cornstarch
½ cup heavy cream
6 large egg yolks, lightly beaten
2 large eggs, lightly beaten
½ cup fresh lime juice
½ cup fresh orange juice
½ cup sugar
4 tablespoons unsalted butter

½ cup whipped cream, or to taste

1. To prepare the pastry, in a mixing bowl, mix the flour, sugar, and salt. Cut in the butter with a pastry blender. When the mixture resembles coarse meal, slowly mix in enough of the egg and water to make dough mass together loosely and discard the rest. (This also can be done using the paddle beater of an electric mixer.) Flatten the dough into a 6-inch disc, wrap in plastic wrap, and refrigerate for at least 2 hours.

2. When you are ready to complete the tart, pre-heat the oven to 400° F.

3. Roll out the chilled dough and fit it into a 9-inch tart pan with a removable bottom. Cover with plastic wrap and refrigerate for 20 minutes. Line the tart with foil, fill with beans, and bake for 14 minutes. Remove the beans and foil and bake for 8 minutes more. Set aside.

4. In a small saucepan over high heat, bring the sugar and 1 cup of water to a boil. Add the lime zest and boil for 6 minutes. Drain and let cool.

5. To prepare the custard, in a mixing bowl, whisk together the cornstarch and cream until combined. Let the mixture sit for 1 minute, then whisk again. Whisk in the yolks and whole eggs.

6. In a large saucepan over medium heat, bring the juices, sugar, and butter to a boil and boil until the butter melts. Slowly, in a steady stream, pour the hot liquid into the egg mixture, whisking very fast as you pour, to combine well. Return the mixture to the saucepan and bring to a boil over medium heat, whisking constantly. Boil for 6 seconds, whisking.

7. Strain the custard into the baked tart shell and spread evenly. Cool and garnish with candied lime, arranged in small clusters around the edges of the tart (1 cluster to a serving). *May be prepared up to 1 day ahead and refrigerated, covered.* Serve with whipped cream.
  Makes 8 servings

desserts

Chocolate Polenta Soufflé Cakes

These individual soufflé cakes are a creation of my assistant pastry chef, Amir Ilan. Based on cornmeal, they puff in the oven and remain firm, except for their centers of pure molten chocolate. When cut, they release steamy clouds of chocolate perfume. Serve them with a generous dollop of freshly whipped cream or a scoop of your favorite ice cream.

1 cup plus 2 tablespoons whole milk
2½ tablespoons finely ground yellow cornmeal
5½ ounces bitter chocolate, preferably Valhrona
1 tablespoon unsalted butter
5 tablespoons granulated sugar
3 large eggs
½ teaspoon baking powder
Confectioners' sugar

1. Preheat the oven to 425° F.

2. In a medium saucepan over medium-high heat, bring the milk to a boil and whisk in the cornmeal. Cook until the mixture begins to thicken. Reduce the heat to low and cook for 8 minutes, stirring occasionally with a wooden spoon.

3. In the top of a double boiler, melt 4½ ounces of the chocolate with the butter and set aside, keeping warm.

4. In a mixing bowl, combine the sugar and eggs. Place over the bottom of the double boiler and whisk until warm (about 100° F.). Remove from the double boiler and beat with an electric mixer until quadrupled in volume. Set aside.

5. Pour the hot polenta into the chocolate and mix well. Add about a fifth of the eggs and fold in with a spatula until mixed completely. Sprinkle the baking powder over the top and carefully fold in the remaining eggs a third at a time. Be careful not to overmix.

6. Arrange 5 buttered ring molds (about 3 inches in diameter and 1½ inches high) on a buttered cookie sheet. Spoon the mixture into the molds, filling half full (or fill 4 individual soufflé molds). Break the remaining chocolate into 4 or 5 chunks. Place a chunk of chocolate in the center of each mold and spoon mixture over it just to cover. Bake for 10 minutes, or until the soufflés are set, with soft centers.

7. To serve, release the sides and lift the rings off, and place the soufflés on individual plates (or serve the individual soufflé molds). Sprinkle with confectioners' sugar and serve immediately.

Makes 4 to 5 servings

menu

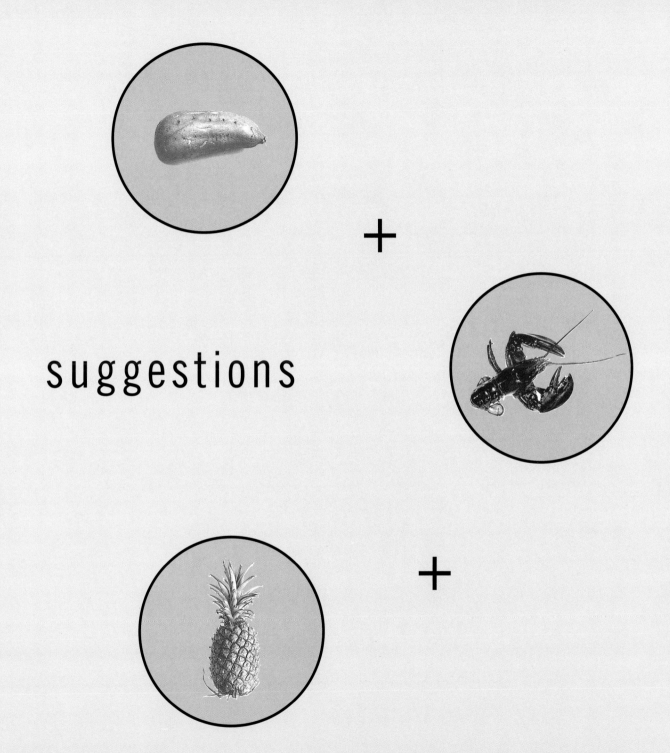

suggestions

+

+

So how do you orchestrate in your kitchen the music i have put down on paper?

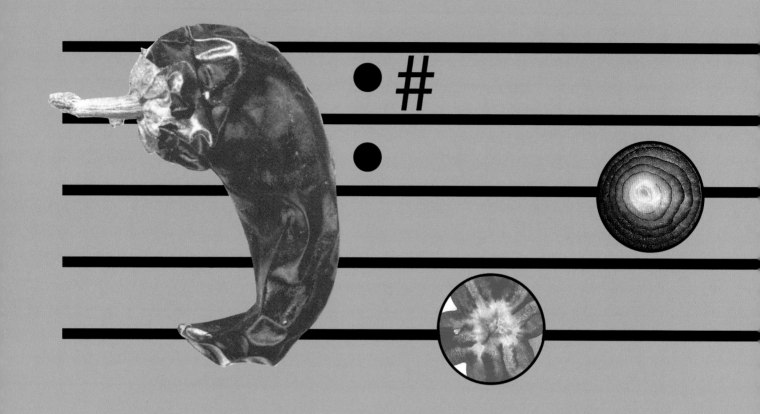

1 song at a time

When I cook Southwestern, I don't dilute the impact: every dish on every menu listed below is a Southwestern special-ty. This isn't just a case of "If one is good, two will be better, five will be great." The dishes I put together truly complement each other.

How do you orchestrate in your kitchen the music I've put down on paper? One song at a time. Every cook knows that meals can be prepared in stages, most things days ahead of time and only very few—maybe one or two—just before serving. I try to explain my menus from that point of view, and I think you will find them really easy when you proceed step by step.

Of course, you are not bound by my choices. You can make a Southwestern dish the spectacular center-piece of an eclectic table and still have a lot of fun. But when you opt for the whole symphony, try the menus here.

Thanksgiving Dinner

Here is a meal that celebrates abundance, with bountiful harvests from the farm and the sea. It features the rich, deep colors of autumn and a lively palette of Southwestern flavors. And best of all, it won't keep you in the kitchen all day. A generous meal like this is usually prepared in stages, many things being cooked early in the week when you have extra time. The chowder recipe breaks down into easy steps; the ingredients can be combined just before serving. You can bake the cornbread and mix the stuffing up to two days ahead and make the cranberry-apricot relish up to four days ahead. The pumpkin bread for the pudding can be baked up to four days early—it's supposed to be stale, anyway—and the pudding finished Thanksgiving morning and kept at room temperature. The tamales can be assembled early the same day and the flavored butter made and refrigerated up to one day ahead or made earlier and frozen.

Pan-roasted squab is a welcome change from the usual slowly roasted turkey; it cooks in under half an hour, while the stuffing bakes beside it in a separate pan. The tamales should be put on to steam a little before the squab, since they take 45 minutes. The kale can be blanched and reserved four hours early, if you choose, or just before the final cooking, which takes all of five minutes.

Menu

- Curried Corn and Fresh Clam Chowder
- Pan-roasted Squab
  with Blue Corn–Chorizo Stuffing
- Cranberry-Apricot Relish
- Baked Sweet Potato Tamale with
  Orange-Honey Butter
- Creamed Kale
- Pumpkin Bread Pudding

Superbowl Party

When you host this relaxed party, you can put everything out on the table at once, pass things one at a time, or let the dishes overlap. The idea is for you to enjoy the day as much as your guests. People can take what they want when they want it—this isn't like a sit-down dinner.

Although you will set a generous table, the major cooking can be done one to two days in advance and the salsas can be done several hours ahead. At the last minute, you only have to fill the serving trays.

Mix the Yucatán marinade and marinate the chicken up to two days ahead, and then grill the skewers just before your guests arrive. Cook the lamb and black bean chili two days ahead and refrigerate it, then reheat when needed. Blanch and marinate the ducks for red chile duck the night before your party and roast them two hours ahead. Heat the tortillas at the last minute, then carve the ducks and arrange platters of duck meat, tortillas, and pineapple-red onion relish so that your guests can serve themselves.

Give yourself a little time early that morning to put together the papaya-tomatillo salsa, avocado relish, pineapple–red onion relish, and dill sour cream assembly-line style, then refrigerate them until just before party time.

Menu

- Yucatán style Chicken Skewers with
  Papaya-Tomatillo Salsa
- Red Chile Duck with Pineapple–Red
  Onion Relish
- Lamb and Black Bean
  Chili with Avocado Salsa
- Smoked Salmon and Dill Quesadilla
  with Salmon Caviar and Dill Sour Cream

Fourth of July
Lunch Outdoors

A number of things can be made ahead for this spectacular barbecue, so the final cooking remains free and spontaneous, as an outdoor meal should be. Prepare the quesadillas, the potato salad, the flavored butter, and the cobbler at your leisure. Mix the marinade up to one week ahead and brush it over the fish two hours before grilling time. That leaves just the corn and the grilling for mealtime.

Menu

- Goat Cheese Quesadilla with Tomato and Basil Salsa
- New Mexico–style Barbecued Salmon
- Southwestern Potato Salad
- Roasted Corn with Chipotle Butter
- Peach and Blueberry Cobbler

Weekend Dinner
in the Country

This dinner includes summer's generous harvest of sweet golden corn and juicy red tomatoes, as well as ripe zucchini, squash, eggplant, and broccoli.

You can prepare the roasted corn soup two days ahead and refrigerate it, then reheat it just before serving. Bake the lime tart up to one day ahead and refrigerate it; whip the cream that goes with it up to two hours ahead. The wild rice also can be cooked two days ahead and refrigerated; reheat it slowly when ready to serve.

Prepare the marmalade for the fish up to one day ahead of time and refrigerate it; bring it to room temperature about an hour before dinner.

Mix the vinaigrette early in the day, but slice the tomatoes and assemble the salad at the last moment. Slice the vegetables for grilling early in the day and refrigerate.

Grill the swordfish and the vegetables at the same time, just before serving. You can easily slice the vegetables into their final shapes and combine them with the heated rice and garnish the swordfish with the marmalade when you put them on the table.

Menu

- Roasted Corn Soup with Smoked Chile Cream
- Grilled Swordfish with Red Onion Marmalade
- Wild Rice with Grilled Vegetables
- Mixed Tomato and Mozzarella Salad with Cilantro Vinaigrette
- Candied Lime Tart

Spring Lunch

Set this light and easy meal on your table using the herbed vinaigrettes (perhaps cilantro or basil-garlic) that you keep refrigerated in squeeze bottles and a salsa that is easily prepared ahead. Bake the crisp early in the day or the night before; mix and freeze the cinnamon ice cream when the spirit moves you. Dress the salad, fry the tortillas, and grill the tuna only when you and your guests are ready to sit down and enjoy this breezy spring meal.

Menu

- Romaine Salad with Vinaigrette
- Grilled Tuna Tostada with Black Bean–Mango Salsa and Avocado Vinaigrette
- Apple-Blackberry Crisp with Cinnamon Ice Cream

Spring Dinner

Blue corn pancakes with smoked salmon and mango crème fraîche start this meal luxuriously and invite lingering over drinks—you had better make extra. You can prepare the pancakes up to four hours ahead and the crème fraîche up to two hours ahead; last-minute assembly will be very quick. The preserves and the flavored butter can wait in your refrigerator. Tamales can be prepared ahead in quantity and refrigerated, either before or after steaming—simply warm them at serving time and top them with the compound butter. The tarte tatin can be made one day ahead and refrigerated, then brought to room temperature before serving. All that remains for you to do at dinner time is fire the grill and cook the lamb chops.

Menu

- Blue Corn Pancakes with Smoked Salmon and Mango-Serrano Crème Fraîche
- Loin Lamb Chops with Jalapeño Preserves
- Baked Sweet Potato Tamales with Orange-Honey Butter
- Mango Tarte Tatin

menu suggestions

Summer Lunch

Aside from sautéing the shrimp for 3 minutes and sliding the quesadillas into the oven to heat and crisp, you won't have to do any cooking for this meal. Build your summer lunch around a harvest of perfect, ripe tomatoes from a farm market. Prepare the pesto up to one day early and put together the quesadilla, as described in the recipe, up to one day before baking. Take a little time, up to one week before, to fuss over the incredible chocolaty cookies and the homemade banana ice cream. Store them separately in the refrigerator and freezer and combine them when you have a minute.

Menu

- Yellow Tomato Gazpacho
- Shrimp and Cilantro Pesto Quesadilla
- Fudge Brownie Cookie and Banana Swirl Ice-Cream Sandwiches

Summer Dinner

Clear flavors and fresh, uncluttered foods add up to a light and summery feeling for you and your guests. But to set this relaxed table you have to do your homework.

Prepare the corn and pepper relish in the morning, roasting the vegetables and combining them with the other ingredients. (You can roast the poblano for the poblano sauce at the same time and reserve it.) Remember to take the relish out of the refrigerator an hour before serving.

You will need 40 minutes to roast the potatoes, but this can be done up to one day ahead of time. Put the tacos together in the morning and bake them (only six minutes' oven time) just before serving. This is when you can whisk the poblano sauce in the blender.

The raspberry custards can be baked up to two days ahead, but save their sugar glaze (if you choose to include it) for the last minutes before serving.

Buy the best salmon you can find for the salmon tartar and refrigerate it no longer than one day. Dice it just before guests arrive. The croutons can be fried early in the day or the day before and kept at room temperature. While you and your guests are busy scooping up the delicate salmon with croutons, the chicken breast can be grilling to perfection.

Menu

- Spicy Salmon Tartar with Cilantro Oil and Plantain Croutons
- Grilled Chicken Breasts with Corn and Grilled Pepper Relish
- Potato Tacos with Roasted Poblano Sauce
- Raspberry Cup Custard with Graham Cracker Crust

menu suggestions

Fall Lunch

Extend the tomato season into fall with this intensely flavored soup. You can prepare it up to two days ahead. You can fry the tortilla garnish at the same time, but you have to dice the avocados and add them just before serving.

For the chicken salad, roast the peppers and beets up to two days ahead and fry the chicken in the morning. Prepare the dressing up to one day early. Slice the chicken, peppers, and beets, toss the greens, and add the dressing at the last moment.

Preheat the oven for the chipotle cornbread and let the pans heat for 20 minutes. Putting the batter together takes only seconds—then put the bread in the oven about 25 minutes before serving time.

The flan is easy to prepare up to one day early; the berry sauce can be made and refrigerated two days ahead.

Menu

- Tomato-Tortilla Soup
- Blue Corn–Fried Chicken Salad with Cayenne-Buttermilk Dressing
- Chipotle Cornbread
- Vanilla Bean Flan with Fresh Berry Sauce

Fall Dinner

I can't think of a more appropriate fall table than this one, with its earthy, smoky flavors and orange-gold colors. Just about everything can be done early—only the game hen requires last-minute cooking, perfuming the kitchen as it crisps in the oven.

Start the soup up to two days early and fry the tortilla chips up to one day ahead. The relish can be prepared up to three days before serving, and dessert can be baked up to two days ahead. The tacos can be layered in the morning and put into the oven just before serving.

You can puree the ancho chiles for the guinea hen up to two days early, and the curry powder for its crisp crust should be sitting in your pantry. Then cook the hens just before serving—they will take under 10 minutes.

Menu

- Sweet Potato Soup with Smoked Chiles and Blue and Gold Tortillas
- Chile-rubbed Guinea Hen with Cranberry-Apricot Relish
- Zucchini Tacos
- Pecan and White Chocolate Tart

Winter Lunch

Save this menu for a blustery, gray day. Nothing is as warming as a steaming bowl of black bean soup, and few sandwiches are as much fun as pork adobo on a crusty cornmeal roll, accompanied by bracing potato chips.

The soup can be made up to two days ahead, as can the adobo marinade for the pork. Mix the aioli up to two days before serving and grill the pork loin just before serving, for less than 5 minutes.

Freshly baked cornmeal dinner rolls are my choice for this sandwich but you can substitute any rolls of good quality. The rice pudding can be cooked and refrigerated up to one day ahead and its creamy caramel sauce can be whisked together two days ahead.

Menu

- Black Bean and Jalapeño Soup
- Pork Adobo Sandwich with Sage Aioli
- Ancho Chile Potato Chips
- Wild Rice Pudding with Caramel Sauce

Winter Dinner

This winter menu warms you up in steps, with its steaming soup, chiles, and freshly grated horseradish. Then it lets you cool down rapidly with a special apple pie and homemade ice cream.

The tomatoes will take only about 10 minutes to roast and the soup will take about an hour and a half. You can prepare it up to two days ahead. The pesto should wait no more than one day before serving, since its fresh quality is important.

You can prepare the mushroom sauce for the filet mignon up to two days ahead of time and grind the peppers for its crust at the same time. Searing the steak will only take about five minutes.

The fresh horseradish can be grated and the horseradish potatoes baked up to one day ahead, covered, and refrigerated. To serve, heat 12 minutes in a 350° F. oven.

The pie dough can be prepared up to three days ahead, but you should bake the pie the same day you serve it. The ice cream can be frozen up to two weeks ahead.

Menu

- White Bean and Roasted Tomato
  Soup with Sage Pesto
- Red Chile–crusted Filet Mignon with
  Wild Mushroom–Ancho Chile Sauce
- Horseradish Potatoes
- Maple Sugar–crusted Apple Pie
  with Vanilla Ice Cream

menu suggestions

sources

+

conversion
chart

+

index

204

Sources

My primary source for fresh and dried chiles, chile powders, canned chipotles, posole, dried yellow and blue corn products, tortillas, and just about anything else Southwestern is a small, well-stocked store in Manhattan's Chelsea section. You can call or write for their extensive mail-order list. It's called:

The Kitchen
218 Eighth Avenue, New York, NY 10011
(212) 243-4433

Try also:
Dean & DeLuca
560 Broadway, New York, NY 10012
(800) 221-7714; (212) 431-1691. Sends products by mail and offers a variety of fresh chiles, as well as fresh herbs, dried chiles, chile powders, canned chipotles, dried yellow and blue corn products, posole, and frozen tortillas. They send fresh tomatillos, when in season.

Balducci's Mail-order Division
1102 Queens Plaza South
Long Island City, NY 11101
(800) BALDUCCI. Will send fresh and dried chiles, fresh herbs, several kinds of chile powders, canned chipotles in adobo sauce, posole, blue cornmeal, and tortillas. They carry many products that are not listed in their catalog, and will send fresh tomatillos by special order.

The Chile Shop
109 East Water Street
Santa Fe, NM 87501
(505) 983-6080. Will mail dried Mexican chile peppers, American chile powders, dried green chiles, posole, and chipotles in adobo sauce in jars, among other products.

Texas Spice Company
PO Box 3769, Austin, TX 78764-3769
(800) 880-8007, (512) 444-2223. Sells a wide variety of dried spices, herbs, and chile products, such as Mexican chipotles when available and pure ground chile powders with no additives.

Carmen's of New Mexico
401 Mountain Road NW, Albuquerque, NM 87102
(800) 851-4852. Will mail dried chiles, chile powders, blue corn products (including popcorn and pancake mix), posole, and tortilla mix.

For Texas caciotta cheese, I rely on the superior product made by:
The Mozzarella Company
2944 Elm Street, Dallas, TX 75226
(800) 798-2954; (214) 741-4072.

For maple sugar, a good mail-order source is:
Dakin Farm
Route 7, Ferrisburgh, VT 05456
(800) 99-DAKIN; (802) 425-3971.

Conversion Chart

LIQUID MEASURES

Fluid Ounces	U.S. Measures	Imperial Measures	Milliliters
	1 tsp.	1 tsp.	5
¼	2 tsp.	1 dessert spoon	7
½	1 T.	1 T.	15
1	2 T.	2 T.	28
2	¼ cup	4 T.	56
4	½ cup or ¼ pint		110
5		1¼ pint or 1 gill	140
6	¾ cup		170
8	1 cup or ½ pint		225
9			250 (¼ liter)
10	1¼ cups	½ pint	280
12	1½ cups or ¾ pint		340
15		¾ pint	420
16	2 cups or 1 pint		450
18	2¼ cups		500 (½ liter)
20	2½ cups	1 pint	560
24	3 cups or 1½ pints		675
25		1¼ pints	700
27	3½ cups		750
30	3¾ cups	1½ pints	840
32	4 cups or 2 pints or 1 quart		900
35	1¾ pints		980
36	4½ cups		1000 (1 liter)

SOLID MEASURES

U.S. & Imperial Measured		Metric Measures	
Ounces	Pounds	Grams	Kilos
1		28	
2		56	
3½		100	
4	¼	112	
5		140	
6		168	
8	½	225	
9		250	¼
12	¾	340	
16	1	450	
18		500	½
20	1¼	560	
24	1½	675	
27		750	¾
28	1¾	780	
32	2	900	
36	2¼	1000	1
40	2½	1100	
48	3	1350	
54		1500	1½

OVEN TEMPERATURE EQUIVALENT

Fahrenheit	Gas Mark	Celsius	Heat of oven
225	¼	107	Very Cool
250	½	121	Very Cool
275	1	135	Cool
300	2	148	Cool
325	3	163	Moderate
350	4	177	Moderate
375	5	190	Fairly Hot
400	6	204	Fairly Hot
425	7	218	Hot
450	8	232	Very Hot
475	9	246	Very Hot

index

index

index